VOICE of BUSINESS

VOICE of BUSINESS

The Man Who Transformed the
United States Chamber of Commerce

Richard Lesher with Dave Scheiber

Indiana University Press

Bloomington and Indianapolis

This book is a publication of

Indiana University Press
Office of Scholarly Publishing
Herman B Wells Library 350
1320 East 10th Street
Bloomington, Indiana 47405 USA

iupress.indiana.edu

♾ The paper used in this publication meets the minimum
requirements of the American National Standard for Information
Sciences—Permanence of Paper for Printed Library Materials,
ANSI Z39.48-1992.

Manufactured in the United States of America

Cataloging information is available from the Library of Congress.

ISBN 978-0-253-02699-6 (cloth)
ISBN 978-0-253-02710-8 (paperback)
ISBN 978-0-253-02723-8 (ebook)

1 2 3 4 5 22 21 20 19 18 17

To my children—Douglas Alan, Laurie Lynn
(so sadly no longer with us), Betsy Lee, and
Craig Collin; my grandchildren—Kathryn,
Sarah, Rebecca, Jennifer, London, and Danny; and
my great-grandchildren—Vivienne, Philip, Kamryn,
Hallie, Nixon, Ada Jane, Charlie, and Sammy.

I am so proud of all of them and they are the primary
reason I undertook this project.

Contents

Acknowledgments

A JOURNEY LIKE MINE is impossible without becoming indebted to lots of people, beginning with Agnes, my wife of thirty-five years, whose love, assistance, and guidance have been essential.

My mother was my guiding light throughout my life. My grandparents were a source of great learning and love in my younger years. My sister, Doreen, was always there for me.

I was so fortunate to have good teachers in my public school education and wonderful role models and mentors at the three great universities I attended: Pittsburgh, Penn State, and Indiana.

My success at NASA, the National Center for Resource Recovery, and the United States Chamber of Commerce would not have been possible without the support of hundreds of staff members and members of the board of directors.

I also wish to thank Lonnie Taylor, Larry Kraus, Meryl Comer, Steve Lebowitz, Jeff Joseph, Bob Kinzie, Carl Grant, Dr. Mike Gaudiose, and Osvaldo Dos Santos for their sincere contributions.

Finally, I cannot fully describe my indebtedness to Dave Scheiber for his exceptional and professional work and who was a real pleasure to work with.

Introduction

I<small>T IS HARD</small> for me to believe that twenty years have passed since I sat down to share my thoughts and ideas in the pages of a book. The last two decades have been a wonderfully full and meaningful period and given me ample time to reflect on the many memorable events in the life I have been fortunate to lead.

For a boy who survived the rigors of a highly challenging, Depression-era childhood in Chambersburg, Pennsylvania, it has been a remarkable journey. The road would one day lead to the heart of NASA when man walked on the moon, and ultimately to the heights of government and public policy with the United States Chamber of Commerce—affording me a front-row seat with seven US presidential administrations, myriad foreign leaders, and key moments in world events during the final decades of the 20th century.

You will read all about that and much more in the book you hold in your hands. But first, I think it would be worth revisiting the theme of my last effort, the 1996 work entitled *Meltdown on Main Street: Why Small Business Is Leading the Revolution Against Big Government*. From my vantage point as president of the US Chamber of Commerce, I felt compelled to make the case against oversized government regulation that had run amok.

Instead of supposedly helping people navigate the challenges of daily life, an excess of rules and regulations was having the opposite effect: increasing frustrations and burdens of the working class. It's amazing how some things never seem to change.

My contention in 1996 was precisely the same as it had been nearly twenty years earlier, when, in 1975, I was named to lead the US Chamber. As I maintained in *Meltdown on Main Street*, "The national spirit of enterprise and initiative has been hamstrung by maddening regulatory red tape and bureaucratic bungling. Laws purporting to help our way of life have wound up harming it."

I advocated strenuously that we must be guided not by an abundance of policy making, but by self-reliance, individual responsibility, and personal initiative. Those principles mirror my own story—the tale of a bold and independent child who came from meager means and faced many difficult obstacles, with nothing handed to him along the way as he charted the course of his life.

Not surprisingly, I feel just as strongly today about the need to push back against big government as I ever did. It is a never-ending fight, and one that began in the early days of our nation, when Thomas Jefferson noted in 1787, "The natural progress of things is for the government to gain ground and for liberty to yield." I have such great pride in our democratic way of life and remain a staunch proponent for restoring the power of the individual and businesses in the face of ill-conceived, poorly implemented, overreaching government programs and policies.

I understand that we also need to be compassionate both as a nation and as individuals. Being anti-big government does not mean we are unfeeling or unconcerned with the needs of hard-working Americans, who are fighting to stay afloat and support themselves and their families. We can give effective help through acts of understanding, generosity, respect, and selflessness—both by dedicated individuals and societal groups, and by fostering in each of us the spirit of self-determination, a core principle of our democracy.

Clearly, certain defined policies and programs are intrinsic to the goals of a democratic society, but in no way is there justification for the government's tendency to attempt to solve all of society's problems and limitations. Such efforts may be rooted in noble intentions but too often fail to address the realities of life and have dismal results.

My belief in the vital importance of business and private enterprise—as opposed to being some sort of necessary evil as many regard it—lies at the heart of my first book, *It's Everybody's Business,* published in 1980. At the time, American business had endured a long period of being beaten down, disrespected, and viewed in a negative light, but it was poised for a renaissance. And I was privileged to have the opportunity to help restore its luster by remaking the mission of the Chamber, empowering it as an effective voice of business, and working hand-in-hand with the administration of President Ronald Reagan amid the dawn of a new conservative movement in this country.

I have been a proud champion for business in America—and an undaunted crusader for capitalism around the world, especially in the late 1980s—a time of profound change in our history when young people living in oppressive nations hungered for a chance to experience personal and economic freedom.

All of this is why I have wanted to document the many steps of my life so that my children, grandchildren, and great-grandchildren—and generations of progeny still to come—would know more about me and the values by which I have lived my life. Even in a book you can't tell the whole story, but I tell quite a lot of it in these pages. And my hope is that the lessons I learned along the way—the value of hard work, facing issues head on and treating others with a kind heart—will benefit anyone.

I also wanted to reaffirm my views on the wonderful system we are so blessed to live in—though I will continue to speak out against big government as long as I can. You will read much about my work on that front in the chapters that delve into my twenty-two-year tenure with the Chamber, a transformational time of working—and butting heads—with numerous national politicians and even a few presidents.

For now, I invite you to sit back and join me on a ride that, by all rights, should never have led me beyond the tough streets of my Chambersburg childhood. But I'm deeply grateful that it did.

Now let the adventure begin.

VOICE of BUSINESS

1   A Meeting in the Desert

*T*HE *E*GYPT*A*IR *JET cruised high above a vast desert expanse of the Sinai Peninsula late one autumn afternoon of 1981. The flight had originated in the United Arab Emirates, the oil-rich nation tucked along the Persian Gulf to the southeast, and now the plane gradually crossed over the Red Sea toward an uncertain welcome.*

The sky was a deep blue on this cloudless day, looking like a picturesque magazine photograph as the packed airbus began its slow descent to Cairo. But the breathtaking, travelogue view below was a stark contrast to the chaotic, potentially violent scene waiting on the ground in the country's capital city.

As the plane cruised over golden silhouettes of a past civilization—a line of pyramids rising from the Sahara—one passenger on board was far less interested in the riveting images of ancient times than he was in his scheduled meeting the next morning with the new leader of a nation in turmoil. For that traveler, the momentous trip was—in its own way—only one small part of an amazing lifetime journey from humble roots and childhood hardship to a central business role on the world stage. The inherent risks involved in the visit didn't deter the man who learned at an early age in a small Pennsylvania town to face fears head-on and never run from a challenge.

Dr. Richard Lesher, in his sixth year as president of the United States Chamber of Commerce, peered out the window and pondered what kind of help he might be able to offer Egypt's new president, Hosni Mubarak. Barely three weeks earlier, Mubarak had restored order following the shocking and brutal assassination of his predecessor, Anwar Sadat, which had been carried out by members of the Egyptian Islamic Jihad during a victory parade on October 6, 1981.

The killing of Sadat—at an event to celebrate the eighth anniversary of Egypt's crossing of the Suez Canal—was a massive setback to peace efforts in the combustible Mideast; but it shook Lesher on a personal level as well. He had developed a warm rapport with Sadat in March 1979, during the Egyptian leader's landmark visit—along with Israeli Prime Minister Menachem Begin—to Washington, DC. The foreign dignitaries had come to the nation's capital to sign the momentous Egypt-Israeli Peace Treaty, witnessed by President Jimmy Carter in an historic Rose Garden ceremony at the White House.

The atmosphere in Washington had been electric, fueled by massive media coverage, and the Chamber of Commerce found itself in the midst of the fanfare. Following a White House state dinner for Sadat and Begin, held in a tent on the south lawn to accommodate the overflow crowd, Lesher hosted a pair of lavish Chamber events in honor of the two dignitaries who now commanded the international spotlight. First came a dinner for Sadat at the Chamber of Commerce Building, where President Carter made a rare appearance to introduce the Egyptian president; then a luncheon the next day for Begin at the Plaza Hotel in New York City with Vice President Walter Mondale representing the White House.

Down-to-earth and always quick with a joke to break the ice, Lesher—known to friends and colleagues by his nickname, Dick—had established a comfortable and easy rapport with Sadat. He had felt more of a connection with Egypt's charismatic and personable president than with most of the heads of state he'd met during his years leading the Chamber. The two men held a private meeting at the Egyptian Embassy and Sadat extended an invitation to come to the Mideast, when the time was right, to discuss business relationships—such as the emerging American Chamber of Commerce in Cairo, ways that the United States. could encourage trade and investment flow by eliminating tariffs or other barriers, and how the Chamber could help the Egyptian economy succeed.

Now, as the flight neared its destination, crossing above the Suez Canal, Lesher's thoughts turned to the meeting that lay ahead the next day. Mubarak, who served as Sadat's vice president and been wounded in the attack, had urged Lesher not to cancel the trip to Egypt after the Chamber took steps to do so. The new president wanted to give the impression to other countries that life was back to normal.

Given Mubarak's eagerness to keep the appointment, Lesher was happy to oblige; but the fact was, he had no clear sense of the man he was traveling to meet—or the dangerous scene on Cairo's streets that couldn't have been further from normal. At that moment, a distraction interrupted his thoughts—the pilot and copilot relayed word that they wanted Lesher to join them. He unbuckled his seat belt, moved to the front of the plane, and pulled aside a simple curtain separating the front cabin from the cockpit—wondering what on earth they could possibly want from him.

I've learned over the course of my life that humor is a common language, no matter what situation you may find yourself facing. I've always made a point of keeping an arsenal of jokes—most of them family friendly and many dealing with my favorite target for good-natured ribbing: lawyers. When I stepped behind the curtain into the cockpit—an unfathomable layer of non-protection even for the early 1980s—the smiles from the two pilots at the controls instantly put me at ease. They had learned from a staff member traveling with me that I had an impending meeting with their country's president. That revelation had sufficiently piqued their interest to prompt an invitation to join them on the final leg of the flight.

They opened a jump seat for me, instructing me to sit down and buckle up—and then followed with a flurry of well-intentioned questions. Who was I? What kind of job did I hold that would warrant a personal audience with the president? Had I ever been to Egypt before? Honestly, I was flattered that they considered me enough of a VIP to have me join them and allowed the good-natured quizzing to continue. I understood why they would want to know more about an American visitor on a flight predominantly filled by Egyptian and other Middle Eastern passengers, considering that their country teetered in such a precarious state following Sadat's assassination.

To my surprise, once I had satisfied their curiosity, we began swapping jokes and having a wonderful time, mitigating my apprehension about the conditions on the ground. If you had asked me before boarding whether I could have imagined sharing the company on the AirEgypt plane with the men flying it, that thought alone would have made me laugh. However, the natural flow of our conversation made for an unexpectedly enjoyable experience.

I remained in the jump seat for the duration of the flight, which, of course, was entirely against regulations. Apparently, the pilot and copilot didn't hold those rules in high enough regard to have me return to my cabin seat. On the final approach, in the midst of our jovial banter, I remember being alarmed by the sight below of bivouacked military outposts lining the perimeter of the airport. But there was certainly no turning back now. After landing, I thanked my newfound friends in the cockpit for the hospitality and made my way into the terminal, now realizing that though I had anticipated some conflict, I had grossly underestimated the fear and tension that held Cairo in their grip.

Soldiers roamed the airport with machine guns and dogs. As I arrived in the heart of the city, riding in a car that had been sent to pick me up, a heavy police and military presence filled the sidewalks in every direction. Given today's fragile state of security and constant threat of terrorism, it seems inconceivable that back then I had such a minimal comprehension of the region's perilous dynamics. At the time, I didn't even know what the word *jihad* meant. I wasn't fully focused on the deep volatility of the world I was entering—instead intent on building a relationship with Mubarak. On this, my first trip to Cairo—and on my subsequent visits—the hosts always provided police protection, so I felt prepared for whatever situation might arise.

Our presence in these American Chambers of Commerce—AmChams—always gave us an effective vehicle to explain to foreign officials and business leaders how their country and ours could work together on trade and investment. My trips gave these AmChams heightened visibility, while their staffs—not always populated by Americans, but by locals—would brief me on whatever issues I'd be facing on a visit with the host government. On a later visit to Egypt to speak with the American Chamber group, someone asked me, "Aren't you afraid to come here with all that is going on?" I responded, not unexpectedly, with a joke—"You have to realize . . . I work in Washington, DC"—and the quip triggered laughter throughout the room.

I've never been one to scare easily—no doubt the result of my experiences during my childhood and teen years. My father was an extremely difficult man; an underachiever and an alcoholic who often beat my sister, mother, and me for merely perceived minor offenses. From the time I was a young boy, he encouraged me to hitchhike in order to save the nickels he gave me for bus money. I guess you could say I had a love-hate relationship with him. I felt constantly motivated to establish myself as a success in order to escape the long shadow he cast on my life, and the sense of shame and embarrassment I often felt because of his behavior. If there was any good that came from his outrageous ways, it was the sense of independence, self-reliance, and fearlessness I developed at a young age to tackle myriad challenges. But more on that in the pages to come.

Perhaps my background helps explain why I didn't have enough sense to worry about this trek into post-Sadat Cairo. Having grown up amid so much conflict—learning to roll with my father's unpredictably explosive, reckless, and sometimes lawless behavior—I came to trust my own instincts. And I developed an inner confidence in my ability to handle difficult and occasionally dangerous situations. In fact, the trip to Egypt was similar to a visit I'd made to Seoul to speak to the Korean Chamber of Commerce and Industry a year or so earlier. I had discovered after that event that the building in which the event took place had been surrounded by military police for my own protection. Despite the inherent dangers, I had never considered not going. Nor had I thought of cancelling my trip to Cairo, even knowing there could be safety issues—a reality that was underscored as we approached my hotel. There was no way to miss the images of a heightened state of alert, with heavily armed soldiers, sandbags, and machine guns at every major intersection.

That night in my hotel, an armed guard kept watch outside my door. I remember asking him if he would be so kind as to reposition himself down the hall by the elevator. "If anyone is out to get me," I joked with him, "you're going to tip them off that this is my room!" They held their position, despite my mild protestation. Though I didn't change my mind about the importance of making the trip, I fell asleep wondering what I might have gotten myself into in my determination to oblige Mubarak.

The next day, my driver picked me up and we slowly traversed the barricades, detours, and checkpoints, finally arriving at the posh presidential summer palace—a majestic building of beige stone—guarded by sand-colored armored tanks. I was ushered to the spacious, elegantly appointed office of the president, where Mubarak, a husky former Egyptian Air Force pilot, was waiting to greet me and eager to discuss business and trade opportunities. My general recollection is that he was not as outgoing as Sadat, but warm and friendly nonetheless.

Our meeting lasted more than an hour, laying the groundwork for a solid working relationship and an agreement to further Egyptian-American business interests. He explained to me that he intended to run a free-enterprise economy, determined to privatize government-run businesses and encourage trade and investment.

In my mind, the greatest accomplishment of the trip was simply the symbolism of being there—more than the actual substance of our initial discussions. For all the buildup, and all the safety concerns I might have been wise to weigh, my visit was relatively brief and largely uneventful, except for one ride on a military helicopter to show me the United Arab Emirates countryside. Having taken off around dusk, and flying at 3,000 feet, the pilot had suddenly and shockingly dropped the chopper down to less than 100 feet. He never explained why he made that maneuver and I still don't know why to this day. Perhaps he was just trying to give us a thrill, but it was a reminder of the risky world I had entered. I left Egypt, following a meeting at the American Chamber in Cairo, with the foundation of a friendship that could one day prove valuable to the US Chamber—and, by extension, American business interests in Egypt as the country regained its equilibrium.

In addition, I came away feeling a connection to the new president similar to the one I'd felt with Sadat, which made the trip more than worthwhile. I visited with Mubarak seven or eight times after that, either in Washington or Cairo. I frequently made a point of challenging him to a friendly game of tennis, one of my favorite pastimes. He always countered with an offer to face me in squash—a sport, he explained, that was far less strain on his knees. We never did play, but I took the opportunity to teasingly reference squash with him during a political dinner function on one of his trips to Washington.

I was sitting next to him at a head table with other members of the Egyptian delegation and, when the conversation had died down, I said to him, "Mr. President, you only made one blunder since you've been in town this week." A hush came over the whole table, and I'm sure everyone was thinking, "What is this man saying to our president? Is he crazy?" Though we had developed a basic friendship at this point, he appeared unsure of what was coming next and replied, with an unmistakable glare, "Oh? What was that?"

"Well, I understand that this morning you beat Senator Heinz at squash," I answered, referring to Pennsylvania Republican John Heinz. "You shouldn't do that, because he's the chairman of the committee that approves your budget."

I admit that it was mildly risky to make the president of Egypt even momentarily fidget at a function in his honor, but I've always found that kidding or giving people fun little jabs loosens them up—and it did the trick here. Mubarak and all the guests at the table burst out laughing, setting a collegial and comfortable tone for the rest of the dinner.

My experience with Mubarak serves to underscore a larger point about the US Chamber of Commerce, an organization I was chosen to lead in 1975 after a painstakingly thorough search for candidates. By the time I arrived, the Chamber—as anyone acquainted with it at the time will tell you—was essentially dormant. It was a stodgy, moribund organization founded in 1912 and anchored in its decades-old past. What the Chamber desperately needed was an injection of new life; someone to break from the old-school way of operating, modernize it, and make it a relevant force on the domestic and international scene.

I wasn't necessarily the obvious choice, as one who hadn't run a Fortune 500 Company or come up through the ranks of some leading manufacturer. But the search committee recognized it was time to engineer a fundamental change in the Chamber's approach, and apparently saw in me a creative and independent thinker who wasn't scared of a fight.

I'm proud to say that in the twenty-two years that I would eventually serve as president and chief operating officer—from 1975 to 1997—the US Chamber of Commerce grew from twenty-five thousand members to more than two hundred thousand members, and turned from a $25 million organization into an $80 million organization. We had twenty-five American Chambers overseas when I began; today there are more than one hundred. Furthermore, I left the Chamber with $50 million in reserves, $25 million in securities, and real estate worth another $25 million!

During my tenure, we became a force to be reckoned with domestically, hosting Presidents Carter, Reagan, Bush, and Clinton, as well as scores of senators, congressmen, cabinet members, and agency officials. We were enthusiastic backers of Reagan's economic policies and his aversion to raising taxes. But when the president decided to raise taxes in 1982, I put my job on the line by opposing him because—much as I hated saying "no" to a leader I greatly admired and respected—I believed it was the right thing to do. It was my job to carry out the policies of the board, and preserving the integrity of the process was of paramount importance. Later, I received a high compliment from Reagan, when he remarked during a speech to five thousand Chamber members at Constitution Hall, "Dick Lesher is the man who is to federal tax rates what Conan the Barbarian was to anyone who got in his way."

I suppose the rough-and-tumble childhood I lived, where you had to be tough to get by, came in handy in times like that. Looking back, the one time my father's advice really helped me as a youngster came during a playground basketball game. One particular bully started fouling me and pushing me around. Finally, he threw up his fists to fight. I remembered what my father had told me, "If you have to get in a fight, make sure you throw the first punch—and make sure it's a good one." When that boy raised his clenched fists, I stepped forward and hit him square in the face. It was a lucky punch, because his eye immediately puffed up and he ran away, yelling, "I'll get you some other day!" Suffice it to say, when you get in a fight with the president of the United States and his cabinet, you need all the training and experience you can muster.

While always focused on improving business at home, we simultaneously looked beyond our borders to encourage goodwill and improved economic relations with foreign governments. It reached a point where almost no head of state ever came to Washington without visiting the US Chamber of Commerce. And whenever the situation called for it, I was ready and willing to travel overseas for the sake of enhancing the nation's economic climate and promoting the American way . . . even if it meant a flight over the Egyptian desert and into a hotbed of unrest to get the job done.

2   Guiding Forces

*I*N LATE JUNE *of 1863, Confederate troops under the command of General George Pickett marched into southern Pennsylvania as part of Commander Robert E. Lee's strategy to defeat the North. Before beginning their eastward surge to Gettysburg, they had pushed across the Mason-Dixon Line into the little Cumberland Valley township of Greencastle earlier in the month, wreaking havoc on local businesses, farms, and food supplies. Frustrated and fearful citizens were powerless to stop the weeks of plundering and carousing. Finally, on June 26 and 27, Pickett led his emboldened soldiers through the streets on foot, on horseback, and in wagons in preparation for a bloody date with Civil War destiny.*

As they traveled along N. Carlisle Street, a seventeen-year-old girl rushed from her family's front porch to the sidewalk, wearing an American flag wrapped around her waist like an apron. Published accounts tell the story of what happened next: The courageous teen, Dolly Harris, waved the Union flag tauntingly at the passing troops. When one officer demanded that she remove the flag, she is said to have shot back, "Not for you or any of your men!"

Dolly continued waving the Stars and Stripes at the advancing army, reportedly calling them dirty traitors and plunderers as they moved by, only several feet from where she stood. When Pickett rode into view and observed the increasingly incendiary scene, with angry Rebels yelling at her, he was concerned enough for the young woman's safety that he stood up in his stirrups, took off his hat, and saluted her—a cue to his men to show proper courtesy in spite of her bold and blunt protestations.

Dolly would eventually be hailed as an unsung heroine of the Civil War, her bravery memorialized in poems and stories of Franklin County's past. She eventually married a Union soldier who had fought at Gettysburg, a man named John R. Lesher.

They settled in Waynesboro, just to the southeast of Greencastle, raising four sons and two daughters and moving to nearby Chambersburg around the turn of the 20th Century. Two generations later, a great-grandson, Richard L. Lesher, was born in the rural valley town of Doylesburg thirty miles to the north, moving with his family back to Chambersburg when he was two.

He grew up rugged and resourceful in the old railroad and manufacturing town, learning to hunt and trap in the surrounding countryside from the time he was a child. Chambersburg became an integral part of his life—a place rich in American history with many frontier, Revolutionary War, and Civil War landmarks; a place that shared a coincidental connection in name with the business organization he would one day lead.

And it was a place where the unflinching independence and fearlessness of his great-grandmother, Dolly Harris, was embedded in his DNA, and became a guiding force as the boy made his way on a daunting road ahead.

When I made my entrance into the world on October 28, 1933, my parents and older sister, Doreen, were still living with my mother's parents, who worked in Doylesburg as chiropractors. This was the depth of the Great Depression, and men would constantly get off train cars at a railroad station two doors down from my paternal grandparents' home in Chambersburg—knocking on doors and asking for a bite to eat.

I was later told stories of how my grandmother made sandwiches for those rail riders, handing one to each of them, along with a bar of soap to clean off the soot and grime from long nights inside the crowded freights. I think of that simple act of hers as my first lesson in the virtues of generosity with those in need, a value that would guide me in my adult life.

I was still a baby when my maternal grandfather passed away, and it wasn't long before my dad, Richard E. Lesher, got the itch to find a place of our own back in his hometown of Chambersburg. As I would gradually come to learn, Chambersburg was a place with a powerful Civil War legacy. It was an area that had served as a stop on the Underground Railroad for escaped slaves seeking freedom, where abolitionist John Brown had stayed in a downtown boarding house before leading his 1859 raid on a US military arsenal at Harper's Ferry, West Virginia, and where Brown and heralded African-American statesman Frederick Douglass met at a stone quarry to discuss the raid that became a catalyst of the North-South conflict. Chambersburg also held the infamous distinction as the only Northern city burned to the ground by Confederate forces, after failing to raise the ransom demanded in July, 1864 by Brigadier General John McCausland.

Of course, I knew nothing of this history for quite some time, or the fabled heroics of my great-grandmother who'd stood her ground against rebel invaders. My family's own tumultuous history in Chambersburg began in a run-down house of which I have no recollection. My father then moved us to a single-bedroom, second-story apartment in a ramshackle house on Second Street, shaped fittingly like an L, as if for Lesher.

That's where I have my first distinct memories—of days filled with nonstop games my sister and I played outside, coupled with the constant air of tension and uncertainty created by my father. Even as a young child, I was aware that we were frequently behind in rent payments, because the landlady often shut off the heat in our apartment and we'd have to shiver ourselves to sleep at night. In our living room, we had a small, portable kerosene stove to generate whatever heat we could get. And it got so cold in the bedroom I shared with Doreen that ice would sometimes form on the windows. I'll never forget how my father came into the bedroom, turned on the light, and looked behind a chest of drawers. We watched him pull out his revolver and shoot a big rat he'd heard scampering around. It had made its way down from the attic door, which was two feet from my bed. He picked up the dead rat and matter-of-factly told us to go back to sleep.

That was my dad—a man who worked sporadically at construction and other odd jobs, but he never seemed to bring home much of whatever money he earned. On more than one occasion, he failed to make payments on products he bought and they'd be repossessed—like our family's cherished Victrola. I remember when a man just came and took it away. And shortly after I turned fourteen, we were evicted when my dad failed to pay the rent, even though the economy had begun to turn around after World War II.

The income we relied on for groceries, rent, and utilities came from my mother, Rosalie, who worked in a sweatshop in town, sewing garments for a clothing manufacturer. My mom was the rock of the family—not just because she had to constantly find a way to deal with my father, but because of the foundation she provided for me, and Doreen, and two more siblings that arrived when I was a young teen. Mom was a beautiful woman in her youth, a former pageant winner as Ms. Doylesburg. Long, grueling hours in the factory dimmed some of her radiance, but she still was lovely, despite all the burdens she carried from her troubled marriage. What's more, she always put food on the table and made sure we attended Sunday school, no matter what.

As hard as it was when we didn't have heat or enough money to cover expenses, we didn't think of ourselves as underprivileged children; many of the families we knew were struggling to get by during those harrowing economic times. The most difficult part of my childhood came when my father drank too much and—in unpredictable fits of anger—beat my mom, or belted me or Doreen with a leather strap. In addition, we'd hear from time to time that he'd been locked up for various infractions. In a small town, *everybody* knows if your father is behind bars. In our case, the shame we felt was even greater, with the jail located only several blocks from our house. I never liked to walk with friends past the tall, bland building when he was inside, sensing that he could see me from one of the tiny windows overlooking the street. It seemed as if everyone in the entire world knew about my father's incarceration—as well as *all* our personal business, which gave me something of a complex from a young age.

My dad never did anything dramatic enough to allow me to brag about his exploits. Making him seem bold and daring might have allowed me to deflect some of my embarrassment, but his run-ins with the law usually stemmed from smaller violations—like the illegal gambling hall he ran in town, or from barroom fights he frequently engaged in, more often than not throwing the first punch.

One day, when I was eight or nine, my father had gotten roughed up by three men during a bar brawl about a block from our apartment. It's one of my most vivid memories from that period. He came home and instructed me to grab my baseball bat and follow him back to the pub, then told me to stand by the entrance with the bat. "If anyone tries to get me from behind," he explained sternly, "you hit them with this bat as hard as you can." He barged inside, with me following tentatively behind, trapped between being frightened out of my wits at the thought of swinging a bat at raging grown-ups or angering my father for failing to obey his command. He turned momentarily when we stepped inside and reiterated that I needed to keep a lookout for anyone who might sneak up on him.

Shouting and fisticuffs ensued and, as it happened, several firemen at the station across the street from the bar heard the ruckus. One peered in the window, and I remember hearing him say, "Oh, it's Dick Lesher again." It was just at that moment that the bartender grabbed my dad from behind, bringing him under control. I thought to myself, "I don't think I want to hit the bartender." So I remained frozen in place by the front door, and my father—who had no beef with the bartender—fortunately gave me a pass for not jumping in and taking up his cause with the bat. My dad was told to leave the premises, and I followed him home in silence, immensely relieved by how the situation had played out.

* * *

My father, in his own unorthodox and unquestionably irresponsible way, also encouraged a sense of self-reliance in me as a child.

About the time of the unforgettable baseball bat and bar incident, Dad landed one of his occasional jobs—working construction on a veteran's hospital in Martinsburg, West Virginia some forty-five miles to the southwest. It was summer, and my mom put me on a bus to spend a few days with him, without question, a trusting gesture on her part. Despite my father's erratic behavior, I was excited about the trip. He was still my dad and, when he wasn't in one of his moods, I enjoyed the time we spent outdoors, hunting and fishing. At the end of the visit, I remember that he handed me $2.50 for the bus ride home, but added, "You know, if you just stand out on the highway and stick your thumb out, people will pick you up and you could save that money for yourself."

The notion of having two-and-a-half bucks in my pocket appealed to my nine-year-old sensibilities, so I set aside any thoughts of potential danger—and the horror my mother would surely have felt—and decided to take my father's advice. I'm sure there was part of me that wanted his approval, and showing my toughness and willingness to adopt his money-saving plan was a way to gain it. I returned home without any problems and with spending money to boot, adopting a new habit of hitchhiking around Pennsylvania, West Virginia, Maryland, and New Jersey, or wherever my pals and I had an itch to travel. My dad had given the practice his blessing, so I saw thumbing rides as my ticket to freedom—over my mother's objections. I even kept a little notebook, starting at age nine, marking down all the many miles I logged.

When I was twelve, over my mother's objections, a friend and I hitchhiked two hundred miles to Atlantic City on a summer day, hanging around the beach and boardwalk for two days—staying overnight in a cheap hotel. My mother was both furious and relieved when we returned, but there was little she could do since my father had no issue with our freewheeling jaunts. One Saturday, a few buddies and I caught a ride to Philadelphia to watch a Phillies game and, on another occasion, we hitched our way to Pittsburgh to watch the Pirates. I rarely encountered trouble, though once I hopped in a car with a man who was dead drunk. By the time I realized it, he was already barreling down the highway, weaving and speeding. My heart pounded, and I worried what I'd gotten myself into. Thankfully, he pulled into a restaurant before too long, inviting me inside. "No, no thanks," I replied, and ran off as quickly as I could, hitchhiking back home in uneventful fashion.

I always hoped that a beautiful woman would be at the wheel of the car pulling over to pick me up. But in spite of my optimism, that never happened. My hitchhiking pursuits came to include Doreen, who was only a year older and also enjoyed the adventure. For both of us, it was a chance to break up the monotony of long stretches of time when we had nothing better to do.

The fact was, we were often left on our own from the time we were six and seven, respectively. There were times, as Doreen recalls, that she'd have to stick up for me if a neighborhood kid tried to pick a fight. "I did that a lot," she says. "There wasn't anything about me that was afraid. That's just the way we grew up—unafraid."

My mom was busy at her factory job and my father was off doing who-knows-what: sometimes in Martinsburg, sometimes Baltimore, or any number of places he'd disappear to for days or weeks on end. The truth is, I don't recall my father ever working a full year in his life. He always managed to get laid off just before hunting season—living off unemployment compensation and my mother's meager paycheck. Then, he'd go back to work in the spring, though only after getting in some fishing during the first week of trout season.

For one stretch, Dad ran a gas station at the far end of town, and one Saturday Doreen and I decided we would visit him. There was a bus stop by our apartment and, when it pulled up, we stepped on, even though we didn't have any money. Instead, we told the bus driver that if he'd take us to our dad's gas station, he would pay the fare. That was good enough for the driver, and off we went. The only problem was that when we reached our destination, Dad was anything but pleased to see us. In fact, he was furious that *he* had to pay the driver for our fare and made us walk back home—more than an hour in the hot sun.

We were disappointed, without a doubt, but by now had learned to brace ourselves for harsh reactions from our father. And we made the best of a bad situation on the sweltering trek home. Doreen spotted a house with a swimming pool in the back yard and no fence to keep anyone out. We slipped around back and jumped in for a dip in the refreshing water, before trudging the rest of the way to our apartment.

One Sunday afternoon, Dad actually gave us money for pony rides at a stable on the outskirts of Chambersburg. We both figured he had an ulterior motive—wanting some private time with our mom, hence his sudden generosity as a means to get us out of the apartment for several hours. But when we reached the stable, we learned that there were no rides that day. Doreen and I knew that Dad wouldn't be pleased if we returned too soon and, if we came home with unused money, he'd demand it back. So, we made an on-the-spot decision. We'd heard that fifteen-minute rides in single-engine propeller planes were being offered that day at a local airfield for a minimal fee. That sounded like an excellent alternative to heading home early, so off we went on foot, since this particular excursion predated our hitchhiking days.

Once at the field, we stood in line for what seemed like an eternity, mingling with adults as best we could lest we stand out as unaccompanied children and be barred from our impending joyride. Just as we reached the front of the line, news came that the plane could not be used—someone had thrown up all over the seats. But before we could despair over our bad luck, a new plane was wheeled into position. We handed the attendant seventy-five cents each, and climbed into our seats. We had an exciting time zooming and dipping high above downtown Chambersburg and, much to our delight, could even spot our L-shaped house. As I recall, when we got home, we made no attempt to hide our change in plans and told our parents all about the fun we'd had. Fortunately, my dad didn't get mad about our decision to spend the money our own way. He was undoubtedly happy that we'd stayed out for the afternoon.

What Doreen and I worried about most were the beatings our father meted out with his strap, often for minor transgressions. Picking up the belt and waving it at us was enough to get our instant attention. Punishment also took the form of forcing us to stay inside the apartment, which, at times, seemed like an even harsher form of discipline. Sitting in a stuffy, one-bedroom apartment after school was torturous for two active children. For the most part, we learned to stay out of his way when he was around, which often meant steering clear of him and just keeping our mouths shut.

My dad could whistle in such a fashion that, if we happened to be playing outside, we could hear him several blocks away. He taught our mom how to whistle his way, too, almost like a quail. When it was time for dinner, one of them would step out onto the balcony and do their special whistle as a signal for us to drop what we were doing and come home immediately. Doreen and I could tell the difference between the whistles. If it was my mom, we tended to take our time and finish up whatever game we were playing. But occasionally, the strategy backfired: Mom whistled and we'd assume the old man wasn't home, taking our time to finish whatever we were playing. But minutes later, we'd hear his piercing whistle and then sprint to the apartment, fearing we might see the belt upon our return.

* * *

We discovered that one way to stay out of trouble was to find odd jobs that brought in money. My sister and I frequently sold waste paper and scrap iron, picked fruit, or shoveled snow to earn spare change. In sixth grade, I got hired at the local bowling alley, setting both ten-pins or the smaller duckpins in the nonautomated lanes. It was hard, sometimes dangerous, work, though I earned five cents for a game of duckpins and eight cents for a game of ten pins, and that could add up to a lot of money for a kid. I'd crouch on a platform behind the wall at the end of a lane, clearing away fallen pins and setting up new ones as needed. But my perch didn't keep me from getting hit by flying pins—sometimes bouncing over from the other alley—and it hurt!

I did that for two or three years, coming home at midnight dog-tired and filthy from dirt and grease. My mother cleaned me up and sent me off to bed, already half asleep. In addition, I learned how to set muskrat trap lines along Conococheague Creek and the thickets in the rural outskirts of town—a skill, along with hunting and fishing—that I learned from my dad and paternal grandfather, George B. Lesher, a retired US Postal Service worker.

I'd get up at 4:00 a.m. every morning before school, ride my bicycle for two miles in the darkness, and make my way along the creek to check the traps, which I'd set up along the banks or at the base of a "slide"—a slippery surface the muskrats created to slide down the banks and flop into the water. It was treacherous in the winter, when you could die of exposure. If you stepped in the frigid water and it spilled over the top of your boots, you might be knocked over and unable to restore your balance. Consequently, I was always extremely careful not to trip or fall in the pitch-black surroundings. I'd tote home the dead muskrats on my bike, deposit them on the back porch, and get to class at the old King Street School just in time to beat the bell at 8:00 a.m. It didn't seem out of the ordinary to me, just life as I knew it.

After school, I'd race home and skin the muskrats the way my father had taught my sister and me, stretch the hides, and let them cure outside our apartment. Then I'd sell them to a local trader for two or three dollars, as opposed to the dollar I'd get if I just brought him the lifeless animal. Muskrats were easy to skin and they were our number one prize, much more desirable than opossums, which stunk worse than skunks. Unfortunately, our dad made us skin them too.

At thirteen, I landed a summer job working on a Hershey ice cream delivery truck, which allowed me to earn a whopping two dollars a day two or three times a week. I wasn't crazy about giving up an entire summer day of fun, but I liked making the money. When I turned fourteen, I was hired part time at an ice cream store downtown, the Kustard Kitchen. The application stated that you had to be sixteen, but I lied and added two years to my age. In the summer, I worked a minimum of thirty-five hours scooping and selling ice cream, while also caddying at a nearby golf course, and doing an assortment of odd jobs to pad my income. During the school year, I'd cut back to between ten and twenty hours—two evenings a week from 6:00 p.m. to 11:00 p.m., followed by mopping up and closing the store, and one weekend day—so I could have time to do my homework. At one point, I decided to join the Boy Scouts, but my father wouldn't allow it: "You're not going to join the damn Boy Scouts—the first thing they'll want you to do is buy a uniform, and I'm not paying for it. Besides, I can teach you more than they can!" There went my Scouting career.

My work ethic took root during those formative years. During the Depression, if you wanted something, you had to earn it. My parents had never bought much for me before my job at the ice cream store, but after I went to work there, they stopped buying me *anything* extra. If I needed clothing or supplies for school, I purchased them myself. One day, at age sixteen, I splurged a bit and bought myself a new pair of shoes. By then, my feet had grown to my father's size and he said, "Let me see those shoes." I handed them to him to try on. He put them on and liked them so much that he kept them for himself—and never paid me a nickel for them. I was upset, but didn't want to take a chance on igniting my dad's unpredictable temper so I never pressed the point.

Believe it or not, he sunk even lower than that several years later. When I graduated from high school at age seventeen, he told me to go downtown to the jeweler and put two dollars down on a watch. "That'll be your graduation present and I'll pay for it," he explained. I did as he said, picked out a decent watch and put down the two dollars to reserve it. In the end, my father never followed through, and I wound up having to pay every cent of it myself. But the up side during these difficult years—often made harder by my father—was that the idea of working, going to school, and getting good grades became embedded in me. I saw it as a part of normal life—and something that would serve me extremely well years later as I continued my education and developed a career.

Sports also played a role in my life at this stage. I took up playground basketball because, as I saw it, becoming adept at the game seemed like a good way to keep from being bullied by older boys. I was never very good at baseball; during the summer, while other kids were playing in organized leagues, I was always working. But I loved playing football and, by eighth grade, I got to be a pretty decent quarterback at the King Street School—mostly because I could remember the plays.

I wound up doing double duty as a player and a sports writer, penning accounts of all the league games for the local paper, the *Chambersburg Public Opinion*, at the suggestion of my school principal. I'd play the game, then go home and write my story from memory and deliver the report to the paper. My work as a cub reporter often allowed me to come to school fifteen minutes late, which was all the incentive I needed.

During grade school and high school, I teamed up with a phenomenally talented African-American running back named Donald "Mike" Waters, and we became good friends. I never detected that anyone disapproved of a white kid and black kid hanging around together, though I'm sure some people did have negative reactions in the less-than-progressive period of race relations in the late 1940s and early 1950s. Our friendship remained strong through the years to come. Permit me to jump ahead briefly to describe our connection.

Mike was an impressive human being. He earned a scholarship to the University of Pittsburgh, but—with no one to provide him with support or advice—he eventually flunked out. He returned to Chambersburg, and might well have been embittered. Instead, Mike got a job with the state of Pennsylvania managing a migrant worker program, and also started an action-oriented organization in 1963. The Chambersburg Community Improvement Association was designed to pursue equal rights in housing and employment for minorities in the area and create educational opportunities for children. I was in the early stages of an administrative career in Washington, DC, and I mentored him and provided business advice any way I could, and was thrilled to see him succeed. Bear in mind, this was still the early 1960s. At our first high school reunion, held at a private club, I noticed that Mike left quite early. It turns out he wasn't sure he was allowed to be there.

When I saw him soon after, I said, "Mike, we're going to the reunions together from now on." I kept that promise and from then on, we attended together, eventually with our respective spouses. As my work life began to take shape, I often called Mike up to join me for a round or two of golf at the nearby Penn National course, and the owner never failed to "comp" us when it came time to pay. I later learned that the owner didn't charge us as a mark of approval for bringing Mike to the golf course. "That's the way the world should work, with no regard to color," he said to me. After Mike passed away in 1999, I was proud to join the board of his organization, which promoted a wide range of programs, including tutoring, a food bank, and aid for first-time homebuyers. I was glad to do what

I could to help foster his vision, which lives on today in Chambersburg with the Mike Waters Memorial Park and a Citizen of the Year Award in his name.

* * *

While football provided the bridge to that special friendship, I was drawn as a youngster to another sporting pursuit. I loved playing pool and got to be quite accomplished, thanks in part to the dubious influence of my dad.

Among his occasional sources of income was the illegal gambling house he operated late on Saturday nights in downtown Chambersburg. To run the sessions, he rented the first floor of a building downtown—a space that happened to feature a pool table. On gambling nights, he'd make a huge pot of turtle soup and serve it up as the card playing and betting commenced among his group of vagabonds. Doreen and I were barely teens and didn't dare come around, but our father required us to show up the next morning and clean up the terrible mess from the night before—dirty soup bowls, empty beer bottles, and all kinds of garbage. The up side was that we had free access to the pool table. Both of us had plenty of time to hone our pool-playing skills, an ability that served me well and provided quite a bit of enjoyment—along with some income—later in life.

Some of my dad's influence rubbed off on me in other ways, and probably not for the best. In one particular instance, when I was fourteen, he told me to go to the creek to tend to my muskrat traps. Unfortunately, the muskrat population had dwindled sharply, and the State Game Commission had closed the season. That didn't deter my father, who decided I should set out my traps anyway. When I told him that it wasn't allowed that year, he replied, "What do you mean? Since nobody else is trapping, there will be all the more muskrats for you to catch!" I didn't want to argue, so I set a trap line as I had done the year before. Then, on a Sunday afternoon, I drove with my dad and one of his friends to my spot at the creek.

As he had envisioned, I was able to trap an impressive haul of muskrats, collecting them and placing them inside my coat. The only problem was that a game warden had spotted me, promptly placing me under arrest for trapping out of season. He grabbed my arm, leading me away from the creek and back up a hill toward the road, where his vehicle was parked. My father had just arrived to see the scene unfolding. He jumped out of his car and yelled at the game warden, "Get your hands off that boy! What the hell do you think you're doing?!" My father ordered me into his car and proceeded to get in a heated argument with the wildlife official, very nearly coming to blows.

Eventually, the warden approached me in the car and asked to see my coat, which clearly contained my cache of deceased critters. I was let off with a stern warning, but my dad beat me when we got home for not hiding the muskrats while I was sitting alone in the car. Still, my father didn't get off scot-free for his part in the ill-advised escapade—the authorities successfully prosecuted him for a number of small violations, and he had to pay a fine.

That was my father—a naturally intelligent man, but one who used his smarts to break the rules and try to beat the system. He became a union organizer with a business card from Teamsters Local 385 for plaster and cement finishers. A strong, rugged hombre, having worked with his hands and arms most of his life, he was even tough enough to serve as an enforcer to enroll people into the union. And throughout his life, his anger could boil over at any moment—for no good reason.

I often wondered what caused such ire in him. I knew he was in a serious car accident as a child and had to have a lung removed—even though that never stopped him from chain-smoking Camel cigarettes. Perhaps the trauma of the accident was a contributing factor. Or maybe it was his mother, Laura Lesher, who made him feel he could get away with anything by always bailing him out when he got in trouble—a frequent occurrence. He dropped out of school in the seventh grade after beating up a teacher, and was thrown in jail the first of many times for punching a police officer. It took several officers to pin him to the ground, battering him with fists and hoses before hauling him away. That was the start of a lifelong pattern of letting his anger undercut any chance of holding a steady job, or being a good husband or father, in spite of intermittent efforts to meet those goals.

On the one hand, he could make bullies run the other direction (and, in fact, many years later I ran into a man who knew my father, and recollected how he changed life in an entire neighborhood for the better by single-handedly beating up and chasing off two-bit thugs who had been frightening people).

And I remember how he stuck up for me when I was stopped while walking home with a buddy late one night from my bowling alley job. A curfew had recently been instituted in Chambersburg during World War II and apparently we were in violation. A police officer spotted the two of us crossing the street and placed us under arrest. We were both released to our parents in short order, but my father was enraged. He took me to the justice of the peace the next day and threatened to break the whole place up, shouting, "You're not going to fine this boy for working! He wasn't out gallivanting around—he has a job!" My dad's righteous anger had an impact on the justice, who relented and let me go with no punishment.

On the other hand, you never wanted to be on the receiving end of his anger. One night at the dinner table, he was talking about this or that, and I reacted to a comment by saying, "Ohhhhhh." I certainly didn't mean to imply that I didn't believe him—I'd never take that kind of chance—but he leaned across the table and thrust the back of his hand across my face, knocking me onto the kitchen floor. I was extra careful never to say or do anything as a child that he might interpret as a challenge to his authority.

I was fourteen by the time my younger brother, Nick, was born, followed two years later by a younger sister, Billie. Because of the age gap, it was almost like we had two different families. I was so busy that I never spent as much time with my new siblings as I would have liked, but I was glad that my father never administered beatings to Nick and Billie the way he did to Doreen and me.

Another event marked my fourteenth year, in addition to the arrival of my brother. We were finally evicted from our L-shaped apartment on Second Street for nonpayment of rent. We moved in with my grandmother, Nilo Meredith, who had just retired as a chiropractor in Lewistown and purchased a small house in Chambersburg. By now, I was immersed in school, earning mostly As, playing football or basketball, and earning spending money from my work at the ice cream store. And I added a new pastime to my schedule: dancing.

Students often met at a diner across the street from our high school; before classes began in the morning, during lunch break, and after school, to show off their dance moves. I'd learned a fair number of steps thanks to my mother and sister, and that sounded like great fun to me—an excellent way to meet and squeeze all the girls. I became a regular in the Jitterbug crowd and developed a reputation as a first-rate dancer, which made my high school years considerably more fun. I had a steady girlfriend for a while, but we broke up when she wanted to get too serious. That was the furthest thing from my mind.

One of my friends at the time was Bob Kinzie. Bob didn't have a dad to raise him and, like me, worked countless jobs. I never could have imagined that he and I would reconnect years later in business. Looking back, I've joked that if there were two boys least likely to succeed, it was Bob and me. "I looked at Dick as a big man on campus and very popular," he says now. "I was just a punk. But Dick was a good athlete and very good in school. And even though I didn't see myself on his level, he was always friendly to me."

My mother never encouraged me to attend college—it simply wasn't something we talked about in the midst of trying to keep afloat financially. My father, on the other hand, actively discouraged me from continuing my education. He viewed college as a colossal waste of time and money. But by now, I felt highly motivated to rise above his negative influence. He had squandered all of his opportunities in life, brought constant shame on our family, and was an ongoing source of agitation in our lives.

I was grateful for the ways he made me tenacious and independent from a young age, but hated the person he was when anger and alcohol took hold. I can never forget the time he hit my mother for some imagined infraction, and I tried to intervene—only to be hurled to the floor as my dad stormed out in a rage. In my late teens, there was the night he showed up drunk at a family gathering, but we locked the door and wouldn't let him inside. That only riled him up further and made him scream louder. Finally, I'd had enough. I went outside and asked him to leave—that nobody wanted him there. Amazingly—and maybe he was stunned that I had called him out—my dad skulked off into the night. Though I maintained a relationship with him in the years to come, I was determined to distance myself from his dark, violent, and underachieving legacy.

That led me to entertain the thought of applying to college. I'd always scored well on high school achievement tests, though no teacher ever talked to me about going to college. Nevertheless, in my junior year, I made an appointment with my high school counselor, who also happened to be my football coach. I said something to the effect of, "I'm thinking about going to college, but I don't know where to start." His contribution was to point to a bookshelf across the room filled with college and university catalogues. "Help yourself," he added, with a tone of disinterest. "If you have any questions, just ask."

I began leafing through the pages of various brochures, completely clueless about what might constitute a good academic choice with an affordable tuition. I knew I didn't want to go to Shippensburg University, because it was a teacher's college and I had no desire to be a teacher. I'd heard of Dickinson College, a fine liberal arts school about thirty miles up the road, which meant I might save money by commuting. But when I turned to the page that listed tuition and books costs, I went no further. The fees were so exorbitant that I immediately put the catalogue down.

I didn't have enough sense to realize I should have been looking at more affordable public universities that might even have offered an academic scholarship. I walked out of the office without saying a word, convinced that college definitely was not for me. Instead, upon graduating from Chambersburg High, I worked fulltime at the ice cream store, made extra money selling magazines door to door, and went to work selling new and used cars at Chambersburg Ford. I was so busy that I didn't have time to think about anything else in my future and perhaps I would never have left town if not for the Korean War.

By now, the war was winding down and I thought it was my duty to volunteer. Much to my surprise, however, I was rejected due to a perforated eardrum I'd recently suffered while horsing around diving from a platform into a lake. The injury didn't bother me at all, but it sufficiently concerned the army to turn me away. I informed my boss at the dealership that I wouldn't be going anywhere, and, in fact, was looking forward to a career selling cars.

About a year later, however, I received a letter in the mail that caught my attention. It was a draft notice to report for a physical examination. I did and the tiny hole in my eardrum had apparently healed in the interim. This time, I passed with flying colors. With a clean bill of health, I volunteered for the army again and, within weeks, was on my way to basic training in South Carolina—and an experience that would ultimately change the course of my entire life.

3 Uncharted Territory

*F*ORT JACKSON HAD *served as an army boot camp for basic combat training since 1917, the year that the United States entered World War I. Named for America's seventh president, Andrew Jackson, the installation in Columbia, South Carolina toughened up recruits with screaming drill sergeants, long hikes in the wilderness, and grueling obstacle courses. But for one young soldier who would eventually pass through the training center—which had processed thousands of soldiers for battle in World War II and the Korean War—obstacles were nothing new.*

Dick Lesher had been surmounting them his entire life.

The camp was slated to be shut down after the surrender of Germany and Japan, but the start of the Korean War in 1950 gave the stark, wooded site of endless barracks a reprieve—and members of the 8th and 31st Infantry Divisions received their training at the camp.

By 1954, the Korean War had been over for a year, but troops were still being trained to serve in army installations in Europe and other parts of the world. Lesher, a fit and unflappable twenty-one-year-old, was one of them, and the physical and emotional rigors he had faced to this point prepared him well for the exhausting demands of basic training. He made it through eight weeks of boot camp without incident, and then was transferred to Camp Gordon in Augusta, Georgia, for eight weeks of Signal Corps training—with the unit that creates and manages communications and information systems for all of the divisions of the US Army.

At Camp Gordon, Lesher found himself competing against a steady flow of college graduates, some from Ivy League institutions, and keeping up with all of them without nearly the effort the others expended. Several soldiers he befriended noticed his natural intelligence and what a quick study he was, and urged him to go to college when he left the army. After being shipped to the White Sands Proving Ground in southern New Mexico, on 600,000 desert acres between Las Cruces and El Paso, Texas, the topic came up again.

A fellow soldier told Lesher he should inquire about taking the college General Educational Development test, as a way of earning college credit before enrolling in a university. Lesher had only heard of the high school version of the GED, and had no need for that since he already had a diploma from Chambersburg High. But the idea of a college GED interested him.

He wasted no time, making an appointment to meet with the troops' education and information officer. The official was glad to administer the exam, explaining that it was divided into four parts and that passing any single section was worth six college credits. "But understand," he added solemnly, "most people don't pass."

Undeterred, Lesher took the test, passing all four parts and instantly earning twenty-four hours of college credits. That was added to the eight hours he would automatically earn for his military service. Suddenly, the idea of attending college seemed far more realistic. And the timing felt right for another reason. He had decided to marry a girl he had met and begun dating after high school. One month before being shipped out to a US base in Germany, Lesher flew home to Chambersburg on leave for a small wedding in 1955. With the responsibility of a wife and plans for children in the future, attending college and opening up new opportunities seemed like a wise course.

Another key event occurred while stationed at White Sands. After qualifying for the college GED credits, Lesher began pondering what kind of career he should pursue, and settled on business or accounting, with the possibility of following with a law degree. He then sat down in the education and information office with a college directory and pored over possible school choices—searching for an institution that accepted GED credits, offered a business degree, and was located in or near a city, where he could find part-time work to pay for school and a place for a young married couple to live.

He found 101 colleges and universities in Pennsylvania, and at the top of the list of public institutions was the University of Pittsburgh, 150 miles to the west. Pitt was a school he had heard about for years and the thought of actually enrolling there was thrilling. He filled out an application and, while on leave in Chambersburg, made the drive to Pittsburgh to take the entrance exam. His grandfather, George Lesher, was so excited that he provided the transportation—both of them marveling at the sight of the campus' towering Cathedral of Learning, known as the tallest educational building in the Western Hemisphere.

"I don't know if I can do this, but let's go," Lesher told himself as he walked inside. His grandfather stayed in the car, reading the newspaper and waiting anxiously. There was no need to worry. Lesher passed the exam easily, becoming the first member of the family to be admitted to college. But as it turns out, he was only warming up.

Thanks to the US military, I had done a complete about-face in my attitude toward higher education. Motivated by the generous load of credits I could amass while still serving, I even took a freshman math course in a University of Maryland overseas program taught by a professor from Heidelberg University, giving me thirty-five credits before I left Germany.

The prospect of attending college after all was exciting to ponder, and that helped offset my rather routine and uneventful peacetime experience in the service. With the Signal Corps, I trained on a decoding machine that was exactly the same technology—as I later learned—that my great-grandfather had used in 1860 for the Union troops. It consisted of a box full of rotors and you had to set the rotors to whatever the code for the day was. If you wanted to know the message, it translated it for you. Meanwhile, I enjoyed getting to know such a wide range of people and personalities at White Sands. We were out there in the middle of nowhere, a mix of Signal Corps trainees and even ballistics personnel firing missiles and warheads on the famous White Sands missile range, where the V-2 was tested in 1946.

Religion had been a strong and steady foundation for me growing up, thanks to my mom and her mother. My faith gave me a sense of grounding in my often tumultuous and busy life, and I had a perfect attendance record in church and Sunday school. Now, as a private first class, and one who always carried a small copy of the New Testament in a pocket, I decided to teach Sunday school for little children of army families at the installation.

That led to a friendship with the Jewish chaplain's assistant, Al Simonson, and sparked an idea of creating a small discussion group that would study the world's great religions. We spoke to the Protestant chaplain, who volunteered to have an open meeting at his house once a week. Five or six of us gathered to discuss primitive beliefs, Buddhism, Confucianism, Judaism, Islam, and Christianity. And it gave the participants a chance to broaden our understanding of other cultures, while exploring the big issues of life with which we all grappled.

In addition to my normal routine and training, I worked part-time in the officer's club as a waiter. There wasn't anything to do at night out there in the middle of the desert, so when I read one day that the club was looking for waiters and bartenders, I went down and signed up. I enjoyed the repartee with the brass, and made a little extra money in the process.

When I arrived in West Germany, I was definitely ready for a change of scenery. My role, along with so many other US soldiers, was to reinforce our military presence in the growing Cold War environment with the Soviet Union and East Germany. One of my most memorable experiences had nothing to do with my army duties. It happened on a trip to Nuremberg, where I attended an overflow Christian Crusade featuring the Reverend Billy Graham. Dressed in a blue suit with a red tie, accompanied by a translator in the same garb, Graham spoke in a huge soccer stadium that had been the scene of one of Adolf Hitler's maniacal speeches to rally Nazi troops and supporters during World War II. I thought about the evil Hitler's words had spread over the same seats contrasted to the love and goodness that filled the air in Reverend Graham's message and felt truly uplifted.

Signs of devastation still lingered around West Germany ten years after the war. I spent two months in Bamberg and another four in Mainz. By and large, the citizens accepted us and were friendly, though a portion of the population didn't seem happy to see us walking around. Much of my job was with the Signal Corps, working the Teletype machine in the message center while assigned to an armored division. In the latter capacity, I had to learn how to drive a half-track, an armored personnel carrier that is a hybrid of a truck and a tank. I likened it to hauling a house—you can't see anything behind you except a giant iron box.

To earn my license, a sergeant in the motor pool instructed me to get inside the half-track and simply start driving it. I was up for the challenge, and immediately steered it down a bumpy road. Moving about thirty mph, I quickly found myself threading the needle between two trees and hoping for the best. Fortunately, I made it through without obliterating either tree and that was good enough for my instructor, whose only words were: "You pass." I got my license, but spent the rest of my time on that base crossing my fingers that I wouldn't have to drive that awkward contraption ever again.

The country still had a long way to go in rebuilding after the constant bombings during the war. In spite of the tense East-West relations on both sides of the Berlin Wall, the duty wasn't overly taxing. A regular highlight was to go off the base at night, drink wonderful German beer, and eat frankfurters in the land where they were invented. On weekends, we took buses or trolleys around the area, and toured wineries and festivals near the Rhine River.

I had a friend from Chambersburg at another post and we took a trip to Paris together. It was great fun until we both got in trouble—typical naïve Americans—on the Paris subway. We'd accidentally taken a seat on the first-class car with second-class tickets, and a French police officer handed us a card, telling us in five different languages, that we either had to pay a fine on the spot or be taken to jail. Rather than waste the day in a cell, arguing our case, we paid up and moved on.

In some respects, I was anxious to get out of the service as soon as I got in. But looking back on my time in the military, I wouldn't trade it for anything—and not just because of the GED credits I amassed and the GI Bill that helped defray costs of my impending education. The army gave me a way out of Chambersburg at a time I needed to broaden my outlook. It allowed me to see the world and get to know all different kinds of people, providing a valuable opportunity to see how I measured up in a hundred different ways. It also gave me a formal type of discipline that I'd never had before—further motivating me to do something meaningful with my life. I also saw so much of the world I would never otherwise have been able to experience: I'd done basic training in South Carolina, Signal Corps training in Georgia, gone to White Sands Proving Grounds in New Mexico, been stationed in the German cities of Bamberg and Mainz—all in less than two years.

I applied for early discharge—after serving twenty-one of twenty-four months—so I could return home to my bride and begin classes at Pitt. My wife was a nursing student from Western Pennsylvania. We'd met at a chaperoned event at a lake outside of Chambersburg one night, a gathering comprised mostly of young men and women. Her mother was one of the chaperones, and I decided to play a little game. I said to her mom: "If I win, I get to take your daughter on a date, and if I lose, my buddy Rich will date her." My future mother-in-law later told me she threw the game to make sure I got the date.

I want to say something here about this marriage. We were young and I was overworked between school and my job, unable to give the marriage the time and attention it needed amid the pressures of my studies and work. That placed a great deal of pressure on the marriage, and it eventually succumbed, though we are blessed to have produced four wonderful children. Out of respect for my first wife and my family, I don't intend to go into any details about our marriage as I move forward in these pages, other than those pertaining to our children. Even amid my long hours and intense work on multiple fronts, I always found time for my kids. I taught them all football, basketball, baseball, and pool—in fact, one of my daughters told me she earned all her extra money in college with a pool stick, beating all the guys on campus. We always made time for a summer vacation at the beach, and my boys and I went hunting and fishing. But when it came to me and my wife, ours was a union that just wasn't destined for success.

By the time I left the service as a corporal, in January 1956, our first son, Douglas, arrived. In short order, we moved to Pittsburgh and I began my first semester of undergraduate classes at Pitt. My father, as I mentioned, was completely against the idea of my attending college, but so was my new father-in-law. He made cracks that he'd wind up supporting me and our young family. He'd been a basketball star in high school and had the chance to attend college on a scholarship, but didn't go. It was clear to me that he was resentful of my decision to enroll in college, and probably felt sorry for himself for not doing the same. Honestly, I was far too busy to be concerned with his lack of approval.

I went to school at 8:00 a.m., got home around 3:00 p.m., changed clothes and then drove to East Pittsburgh, where I'd landed a job as a production coordinator with Westinghouse Electric. My shift lasted from 4:00 p.m. until midnight and I'd return home around 1:00 a.m. with just enough energy to shower, go to sleep, and start all over again the next morning. But I had the confidence in myself to handle such an exhausting schedule because that is what I always did, from the time I set pins in the bowling alley each night in grade school.

At Westinghouse, I merely followed an advanced version of the same draining routine. I worked forty hours a week one week, followed by a forty-eight-hour week—and still managed to do my homework and perform well in all my classes. But this still required creating and adhering to a highly organized system to keep me from falling on my face.

My division of Westinghouse involved manufacturing massive generators. The production coordinators during the day shifts were under such stress that many of them quit, and several were reported to have committed suicide from the pressure. When I arrived for the evening shift, my daytime counterparts usually handed off the one job that was driving them crazy—sometimes adding up to a half-dozen challenges to solve when I went on duty. I'd made friends with an employee who drove an industrial truck inside the factory, and together we made the rounds, covering the whole plant—a full mile-and-a-half of it. I got to know all of the overnight foremen, allowing me to deliver to them anything that needed emergency attention. By the time the day shift managers arrived for work, everything was already fixed and waiting for them—something that made me quite popular in their eyes.

In the meantime, I formulated a routine that allowed me to get all my school assignments done while on the job. In my first several hours at work, I'd organize all of my jobs and then sit inside one of the offices to study. For those few hours, the man with the industrial truck—per our arrangement—drove through the factory, tracking both his jobs and mine throughout the evening. When he was finished, I'd usually have my homework completed and could devote full attention to my production coordinator role. It was a tricky balancing act, to say the least, but I was able to make it through with no major hitches.

At the same time, the more success I enjoyed in school, the more excited I became at the prospect of earning my degree—especially since college represented uncharted territory in my family. The idea of higher education seemed so wonderful and attainable that it drove me forward, fueled by the same spirit of independence I had developed as a youngster. I followed the fabled words of Yogi Berra, who uttered, "If you come to a fork in the road, take it." (And, as it turned out, the fork would one day lead to meeting and having dinner on more than one occasion with Yogi himself!) My philosophy was to forge ahead, no matter what, in pursuit of personal progress and achievement. And I kept surprising myself as I went, because I'd often felt slightly inferior to many of my counterparts with a more polished pedigree or better academic background—coming from families where they were taught how to study.

As a side note, one of my big projects was a paper I wrote on fracking in 1957—well before it emerged as a common practice. I'd never heard of the process of drilling deep into the earth to obtain natural gas and oil from shale rock, but I soon learned about it from an older gentleman who worked for Westinghouse. He lived near Pitt's campus in Oakland and I began driving him the eighteen miles to the factory in East Pittsburgh, because he was uncomfortable making the drive himself. By day, he worked as a "wildcatter," the term given to people who drill in old oil fields thought to be dried up.

This man had a business buying old wells that had gone dry, allowing him to frack—essentially *fracturing* the rock with pressurized liquid. If he was lucky, he could draw several barrels of oil a day for a year or more. I had an assignment to write a paper on a topic of interest, and—inspired by all this fascinating new information—fracking seemed like a logical choice. My professor had never heard of the term, which is probably one reason I received an A. I guess you could say, thanks to my old carpool friend, I was way ahead of my time!

My initial goal at Pitt was to earn an accounting degree so I could become a certified public accountant, followed by a law degree. But accounting bored the heck out of me, so I switched to major in finance. And I soon learned that a finance background was the best way to understand a corporation and our economy—a cornerstone for the career path I would one day take.

* * *

I graduated from Pitt in two and a half years, with the help of my GED and military credits and fulltime summer school load. As graduation neared, Westinghouse had me take several IQ tests. I apparently scored well enough to be offered placement in the company's advanced management program. But I thought, "I don't want to spend the rest of my life in a factory, even if I have a shirt and tie on."

One day, I was busy relating my dilemma to a professor, who responded, "Why don't you go on for your master's?" By now, my wife had given birth to our second child, Laurie, in February 1958, and I doubted I could support my growing family while going for an advanced degree. But the professor had attended Penn State University and offered to help get me a teaching assistantship to create an income flow.

I still had one semester of money left on the GI Bill, so the idea seemed entirely workable. Furthermore, I was so delighted to have earned my BA at Pitt that the notion of adding a prestigious MA from Penn State held tremendous appeal. In August 1958, off we went to State College, where I began work on my master's in business. Penn State had such a beautiful, sprawling campus and I couldn't wait to get started in the program—though I took a little needling from my Pitt friends for switching to Penn State, due to the natural football and basketball rivalry between the Panthers and Nittany Lions.

My family was proud as could be that I'd graduated from Pitt. Even my wayward father attended commencement ceremonies, which surprised me to no end but also pleased me that he made the effort. And moving on to Penn State was something neither they nor I had ever imagined. I spent the next two years, including attending summer classes, on my degree. In addition, I taught finance and data processing, and worked the summer of 1959 in Endicott, New York with IBM, including five weeks of training and seven weeks in the field.

I felt driven to push myself, as I'd done my whole life, and prove I could out-work and out-perform others who'd perhaps had an easier road than I did. I found a perfect outlet for my competitive juices when I took part, along with a group of trainees, in the IBM Business Games. We competed against various other teams—figuring out hypothetical solutions to business challenges—and my group won. Later that year, I was elected president of Penn State's team, set to take part in the first-ever IBM National Championship Games.

Each team was placed in a room and given limited financial information. We had to make decisions about production, advertising, and related business issues and hopefully impress the committee of judges with our course of action. The philosophy I followed was based on the same one IBM employed every day: spend a *lot* of money on research, development, and marketing, and let the production side catch up. Adhering to that approach, we beat a number of other schools, and then traveled to Chicago for the championship round.

A pair of professors were assigned to each team, but it gradually appeared to me as if some of the professors were meddling too much. I noticed how they were constantly coming in and out of the rooms, tipping off the opposing squads about what the other was talking about. When the first day of competition came to an end, we were trailing, though starting to catch up—and I believed that our own professors had hurt our efforts by trying to sway us to their way of thinking. That night in the bar, I found them and chewed them out, saying something to the effect of: "You came in there and told us to change our philosophy, and I argued against it. But you persuaded the team to go your way, and you were wrong! We found out we were right all along and we went back to our philosophy. You guys almost cost us the ballgame!"

On the second day, we completed our comeback and wound up as co-national champions with the University of Illinois. And what a thrill it was to see our trophy eventually sitting alongside the Penn State football team's Liberty Bowl Trophy from that year.

During this time, I also served as president of the Graduate Student Club and Graduate Finance Club, leading to my chairing the annual Christmas party—a long tradition in which the graduate students host the faculty members and their wives. I decided to write a play for the occasion: a parody of all the time-wasting meetings the faculty attended. Word leaked out of what I had in mind, and the department head called me in and warned me that I could get in trouble if I insulted our highly strict, straight-laced dean, named Ossian McKenzie. But, I thought, what was the harm in a little playful ribbing? I went ahead with the script, revolving around a meeting of multiple Santa Clauses at the North Pole.

The play—featuring an easel of caricatures of various faculty members—began with a serious, dour-looking Santa intoning with no emotion: "This meeting is called to order by Ossian Claus with a roaring ho-ho-ho." Fortunately for me, the dean, seated near the front, immediately broke out laughing—and that brought the house down. I was always a risk-taker at heart, and I'd come to see that the humor was a terrific way to break the ice and defuse tension—even if some people thought I was crazy for taking the chance.

In retrospect, I may have over-stepped a bit in another aspect of the party. There were always two punch bowls for the affair, one with vodka and the other just juice. But we spiked both bowls. The assistant dean's wife, never a particularly friendly person, was suddenly acting uncharacteristically sociable and happy, having unwittingly consumed the potent concoction. I don't think the faculty or their wives ever realized what we'd done, and I might have had a hard time explaining that one if they had. It certainly wasn't a prank I revealed when I took a part-time job in the summer of 1960 in Penn State's main administrative office, as my master's program neared completion.

By now, my wife and I welcomed our third child into the world, a daughter named Betsy. When I earned my degree in August 1960, my master plan was to teach finance at a good university and build a financial consulting and investment advisory firm. That's when the idea of pursuing a doctoral degree entered the picture. On occasion, deans from other universities visited our campus, recruiting Penn State master's candidates for their doctoral programs. As it happened, I found myself being recruited by both the University of Illinois and Indiana University. Penn State had faculty members from each of those schools, and they lobbied me to pick select their respective institutions. What tipped the scale in my mind was the Indiana recruiter's assurance: "You'll never have to worry about money if you go to Indiana and do well. They'll make sure you can afford it."

My choices had expanded by then, with Harvard University accepting me into its program. But Harvard essentially wanted me to sign away my life savings for the next fifty years, so it was an easy call. I accepted Indiana's generous offer of financial assistance and moved the family to the heartland, where—at age twenty-seven—I began my studies in the fall semester of 1960. Once there, I proceeded to tackle the most difficult challenge I'd ever faced in my life.

* * *

I took a full doctoral load of five courses, taught an undergraduate class in introduction to business and worked fifty-two hours a week as a night watchman. And somehow I didn't collapse in the process.

Even I have to admit that this schedule was off the charts. But, since my money from the GI Bill had run out, I felt that I needed to keep the money coming in to support my wife and three young children, something my father hadn't ever done with any consistency. Furthermore, I was never one to shy away from burning both ends of the candle—again, by choice, the mirror opposite of my dad. I managed to pull it all off in the following manner:

I came home from school, changed clothes, grabbed a dinner bucket to take with me, and drove to the nearby Ralph Rogers construction company, where

I worked thirteen-hour overnight security shifts starting at 6:00 p.m. My first hour on the job was reserved for minor tasks, followed by making full rounds in four or five buildings and a stone quarry. I wore a time clock around my neck and punched it at every location I inspected, as proof I was doing my job. Then, I'd return to the construction office and study. By midnight, my brain was usually on overload and unable to absorb any more information so, from about 12:00 a.m. until dawn, I'd make the rounds every hour, setting my alarm so I could take thirty-minutes naps in between, repeating that throughout the night. By 7:00 a.m., I'd return home, take a shower, and drag myself off to class.

The bottom line in this crazy arrangement: I could only get in bed every *other* night to sleep, hitting the sack at 8:00 p.m. and sleeping for twelve hours to recharge my batteries. Not surprisingly, the enormous grind was taking a toll. And my work at Ralph Rogers came to an end after five months. My boss had promised me that he would split the job into two shifts, and I had a friend lined up to take one of them. That never happened, so I quit. But my decision to leave coincided with a call to my doctoral advisor's office. I had received three As and two Bs the first semester and he was furious with me.

"You don't get Bs in the doctoral program," my advisor scolded me. "You just don't!"

"It won't happen again, because I've quit my job," I assured him.

"You're not *teaching* anymore?" he replied with a tone of utter surprise.

"Not that job—my job as night watchman," I replied.

He looked incredulous. "Wait. You work as a night *watchman*?"

I conveyed to him the schedule I'd been maintaining and he was speechless. But as we talked, he understood my level of commitment to succeeding in the program and providing for my family. And from that point forward, he became something of a guardian angel for me. If any job opened up, he always told the hiring manager, "Give it to Lesher." When it finally came to the dissertation level, I planned to pick a finance subject that interested me, but the dean pulled me aside. He said the school wanted me to tackle a long-range study that would help them—the general topic of non-profit research institutes in the United States and how to best manage the research they conduct.

Herman B Wells, the school's longtime chancellor, was a larger-than-life figure in academic circles back then and a past president of the university. He decided to sit in on my dissertation committee—the only time he had ever performed that role. It was an incredible honor for me. (As an aside, whenever I ran into him later, he'd anticipate my question and reply, "Don't ask, Dick, yes, you're *still* the only one I've ever done that for.")

The specific thrust of my dissertation was to study research management as carried out by independent, nonprofit research institutes nationally. Indiana University had been awarded one of the first contracts by the National Aeronautics and Space Administration to disseminate NASA technology. The university was helping NASA establish the Aerospace Research Application Center, one of eight centers around the nation to promote the transfer of technology to industry and businesses that needed it, ultimately benefitting everyday consumers.

The dean of Indiana's business school, Dr. Art Weimer, had stepped down and had started running the Aerospace Research Application Center. I became his executive assistant, which allowed me to research and write my dissertation, as well as preparing reports for the school's President and Chancellor in the area of research management. That gave me the depth of knowledge and information I needed to write a strong thesis—one that ultimately earned approval by Chancellor Wells and the committee and secured my degree. Looking back, I was so fortunate to have both Dr. Wells and Dr. Weimer as mentors.

By 1961, we had been blessed with our fourth child—a second son, Craig. One of my proudest achievements, especially in these times when there is so much talk about student loans and student debt, was earning a bachelor's degree, a master's, and a doctorate without any financial support from my family and with *zero* debt—in spite of the fact that my G.I. Bill assistance ran out early on. Outside of that, nobody ever gave me a nickel for my education: not my father, not my father-in-law, or anyone else. And just as my army career had been packed with formative experiences from multiple locales, my educational journey had been one for the books. It's far easier to earn three degrees from the same university than it is to get three degrees from three different institutions—you have to learn the whole culture, process, and regimen all over again at each school. Ultimately, the challenge of adjusting to new surroundings proved to be immensely beneficial in my career development at uniquely different organizations—and always helped me get the job done.

My immediate goal was still to teach finance the rest of my life and build a consulting firm. I had interviewed at nine or ten universities as I completed work on my doctorate in 1963: places like Kansas, Kansas State, and Connecticut. But I wound up accepting a professorship at Ohio State. Landing a job at a Big 10 school right out of a doctoral program was a real feather in my cap. And what a wonderful career I felt I'd just begun. I loved teaching and my classes included corporate finance and personal finance. In addition, I started my consulting firm right away, earning as much money from that as I did as a professor in that first year.

But I'd also gotten to know several NASA people from the work on my thesis. And an administrator there, George Simpson, asked if I would come to Washington, DC, for a week over Easter vacation and help write a report for him for a government agency based in North Carolina—a project he was overdue in completing. It sounded like a nice change of pace, so I took him up on the offer and wrote his report. Apparently I did a decent job, because Simpson contacted me again with an idea: "Why don't you take the summer off? Our technology transfer program is the only part of the agency that is not going well. You could come down for the summer and straighten it for us."

I agreed, but almost immediately he asked if I would consider taking a one-year leave of absence from Ohio State to tackle the challenge.

I had just begun establishing roots in Columbus and its outstanding university when I suddenly found myself at a crossroads: one path leading to the university career I dreamed of and the other to the mystique of space innovation.

So I followed the sage advice of the great Yogi Berra about coming to a fork in the road—and took it.

4   Shooting for the Moon

On a brilliant blue summer morning in 1969, one month before a massive crowd descended on a New York farm for the Woodstock music festival, a far different kind of throng gathered on Florida's Atlantic coast. With the eyes of the nation fixed on television sets across the land—and an estimated one million spectators packing highways and beach communities near Cape Kennedy—Apollo 11 prepared for a 9:30 a.m. liftoff into history.

Only eight years earlier, President John Kennedy had set the high stakes in a speech to Congress—that before the decade was done, the United States would land a man on the moon and return him safely to earth. And now that mission was nearly underway on Launch Pad 39, where astronauts Neil Armstrong, Buzz Aldrin, and Michael Collins had boarded the spacecraft some three hours earlier and awaited the final countdown.

Dick Lesher was in the second year of his business doctoral studies at Indiana University when Kennedy made his famous pronouncement. He never imagined at the time that his career path would take him into the heart of the organization responsible for fulfilling the president's wishes, NASA. But here he was on the morning of July 16, peering toward the distant Cape from some three-and-a-half miles away amid a sea of excited onlookers—and feeling a keen sense of investment in the moment.

He had spent the past five years at NASA, climbing to one of the top administrative roles during the organization's race to beat the Soviet Union to the moon. There was no question that he would travel to Florida to witness the launch in person. But Lesher didn't arrive with an official delegation or stay in a posh hotel with other top NASA officials. He flew to Florida with his two boys, thirteen-year-old Doug and eight-year-old Craig, and one of their pals from across the street in their Northern Virginia neighborhood. The boy's father had asked if there was any way his son could go along. "Absolutely," Lesher told the appreciative dad.

Every hotel within two or three miles of Cape Kennedy was booked, and the only way for Lesher and his youthful entourage to get a room was to rent one from a private homeowner—one of many local residents trying to cash in on the influx of visitors. He and the three boys stayed in a basement the night before, then traveled early that morning to the visitor's center and found a spot in the VIP viewing stand, some three miles from the launch pad.

Lesher had attended the launch of Apollo 8 the year before—with astronaut Frank Borman circling the moon without landing. But this launch was different— it was history. He and the three young boys listened, along with the eager crowd, as veteran NASA announcer Jack King provided the commentary over speakers set up at the site, counting down the final seconds—"Three . . . two . . . one . . . zero . . . we have ignition." Suddenly, there was the sight of the fireball at the tail end of the 363-foot-tall vehicle, followed by the shaking of the earth around them from the shock waves and a deafening roar traveling across the barren sand. Then came the unforgettable sight of the Apollo 11 seemingly walking up the launch pad tower, fighting inertia and slowly rising skyward, propelled by the massive force of a Saturn V rocket.

Lesher said a silent prayer as the spacecraft rocketed into the sky, remembering all too well the tragic deaths only two years earlier of astronauts Gus Grissom, Ed White, and Roger Chaffee in a pre-launch test of Apollo 1 when the interior of their command module caught fire. But as the vessel soared out of sight without a hitch, Lesher breathed easier and soaked in the awestruck expressions of his boys and their friend.

In a way, his career had been rocketing through the stratosphere for the past five years. But unlike Apollo 11 and its fabled lunar module that would rivet the world's attention four days later, he wasn't sure now where he would be making his own landing. And it still was hard to believe the unexpected twist that had brought him to NASA—putting his life on an entirely new trajectory—in the first place.

I had to think long and hard about taking a one-year leave of absence from my professorship at Ohio State after essentially just arriving on campus. But I looked at the chance to spend a year with NASA, helping them sort out their one troubled program—technology transfer—as both a challenge and a way to expand my base of knowledge. I explained my circumstances to my department heads and got their blessing to take the year in Washington, DC, allowing me to apply my growing expertise to the space administration. They thought it would be excellent exposure for me and I fully planned to return to the classroom in Columbus a year later.

By now, President Kennedy's commitment to put a man on the moon and bring him back alive before the end of the decade was in full swing, in spite of the national tragedy of his assassination in 1963. Some $5 billion a year was now being spent on NASA projects, supported by nearly two hundred twenty-five thousand people—including thirty-five thousand civil servants, one hundred eighty thousand in industry and some in universities. It's important to remember that there had been tremendous opposition to NASA in some quarters. People thought we were wasting money in outer space when we had so many pressing needs at home. One of the responses to that concern was the spin-off of technology that would come out of the process of putting a man on the moon.

Against that backdrop of some debate over space exploration, and disarray of the technology transfer initiative, I signed on as a consultant reporting to Breene Kerr, NASA's bright new assistant administrator for technology utilization. Breene was a graduate of the Massachusetts Institute of Technology and son of late Oklahoma Senator Bob Kerr, who chaired the Aeronautical and Space Sciences Committee from 1961–63. Senator Kerr was a close friend of President Lyndon Johnson and NASA administrator James E. Webb. Sadly, the senator died of a heart attack January 1, 1963 and—one year later—his son joined the space program that his father had championed.

Breene was personable and clearly talented, and we got along extremely well from the start in our efforts to jump-start the technology transfer program, which was in shambles when we started. The program was Webb's brainchild and basically existed as a side benefit of the agency, designed to accelerate the transfer of NASA technology to society: specifically, to the medical community, colleges and universities, and companies. This endeavor required cataloguing all the new technology flowing from the space program, and then putting it in a form for private industry to find, utilize, and make available to the public. This is how the space program truly paid for itself many times over in the years to come.

Given the extraordinary amount of research and development taking place—all with a sense of urgency in the historic quest to reach the moon by the end of the decade—virtually all of science and technology had to be pushed ahead because something of this monumental nature had never been done before. NASA had made a high priority of documenting the many space-related innovations to ensure they weren't lost and, furthermore, could be helpful in non-space application. That was my job, and I thoroughly enjoyed the work of bringing NASA innovation to the marketplace—an undertaking that would have a lasting impact on products we rely on and have come to take for granted.

If you look around today at many commonplace items, you won't see a label reading, "Created by NASA." But if you explored the history of those items, there's a good chance they were influenced by NASA technology—from such mundane goods as paints and sealants to sophisticated commodities such as computers and the micro-miniaturization of medical equipment. People think of it as NASA technology, but it really was industrial technology—often pulled together from several existing technologies, and improved upon by NASA to create a new product and satisfy the space program's needs.

Keep in mind, astronauts underwent intensive monitoring of their vital signs in the 1960s and the equipment had to be perfectly sound, with what we called "zero defects" in primary and backup systems. Redundant systems were critical due to the harsh environment in outer space, temperature-wise and pressure-wise. For that reason, products such as adhesives and engines had to be more effective than ever before. They also had to be lighter and smaller than ever. Consequently, NASA put forth tremendous effort to create the best and least cumbersome equipment, leading to breakthroughs in lighter-weight monitoring devices that flowed into doctor's offices and hospitals across the country, benefiting all of medicine from that time forward.

One of the first steps I took was to start a number of publications on the topic of technology utilization. One of them was a short and simple tech brief. If a new fastener was invented, for example, we'd create a one-page document explaining what it was, how it worked, and why it was better than anything out there before.

As an aside, many people believe that Teflon was one of the offshoots of the space program that helped us in everyday application, but just for the record, the stick-free substance was already on the market. NASA did incorporate it early on, creating a popular misconception that Teflon sprang from the space program. But what NASA did do, on a regular basis, was issue specifications of what it needed and industry responded by either trying to find it or inventing it. This amounted to a gigantic new technology start-up program—and a constant air of excitement inside the building that was palpable every single day.

To suddenly be playing a role, at only thirty-one years of age, was heady stuff to say the least. That said, I'd make a commitment to Ohio State and in 1965—at the end of my year at NASA—I began making plans to return to teaching. When I informed Kerr of this, however, his response was, "No, you're not going. I'll make you a civil service appointment as deputy assistant administrator of technology utilization if you stay."

That was the last thing I'd expected to hear. But I found the work stimulating, and the job title and pay increase sounded appealing. I thought to myself, "I could do this for another year." So I arranged a second year of leave at Ohio State, relieved that my superiors at the school were willing to extend my leave. My work at NASA in an expanded capacity continued to be incredibly rewarding and, as my third year with the organization neared in 1966, I had a major decision to make.

I could either return to Ohio State to resume my teaching career and consulting business in Columbus, or accept a job offer to become job NASA's chief economist. By now, I felt so immersed in our technology transfer assignment that I decided, after pondering my options, to remain in Washington—albeit with a tinge of regret in walking away from the teaching career I'd envisioned. I sent my letter of resignation and accepted the economist position. I did so, however, without conferring with my boss. And when he learned I'd be moving to the policy side of the organization, he once again wanted to hear nothing of my plans to leave him. "We're tearing that up—you cannot leave me," he told me.

By now, Kerr had taken on a second title, assistant administrator for policy planning, and was willing to offer an enticement to keep me on board. "I'll give you the technology hat and let you wear it," he said. Long story short, I was chief economist for one day. And that's how I came to be, at thirty-three years old, the assistant administrator of technology utilization for the biggest and best government program ever put together. I felt as if I had the best job in the world. Just like that, I had been elevated to NASA's second level, among roughly forty of us running the whole space program—from manned space flight to deep space probes. And I was about fifteen, twenty, even thirty years younger than most of them, which is why many have long since passed away by now.

The top management people I worked with were always very respectful, even with our age gap. But some of the old-line bureaucrats who gravitated to NASA from other government agencies, spending years to get to their positions, were very jealous and I could feel that pressure, but I just worked through it.

In my new assignment, I was responsible for three divisions: Management Information Systems, Scientific and Technical Information Systems, and the Technology and Utilization Division. The first two divisions managed advanced computer-based information systems for NASA's thirty-five thousand employees and thirty-five thousand contractors, and an additional 250,000 people if you included workers in private industry and universities.

It was the responsibility of the technology utilization division to input technical reports from contractors and the NASA centers—and then to output reports to such academic-based contract centers as Indiana University, Wayne State University, the University of Connecticut, the University of North Carolina, and my alma mater at Pittsburgh. Here's how it worked: the application centers signed up local companies in the respective states to join our network, and those companies would be serviced by the participating universities if they encountered technical problems.

My wife and our growing family of two boys and two girls lived in a nice subdivision of Annandale, Virginia, a fairly easy commute to downtown Washington if you didn't get caught in the area's notoriously bad traffic. All told, I had about one hundred fifty people working for me, and another two thousand on a contract basis. In addition to the well-known manned space-flight centers in Houston, Cape Kennedy, and Huntsville, there were about fifteen other centers in places such as Ohio, Virginia, and California. I had people who reported to me in all of those areas, galvanizing the process of putting the technology into the system so it could be made available to the public at large.

One of my key hires at this time was a prolific and brilliant technical writer named George Howick, who served as director of the technology utilization division. Howick had been kicked out of college his senior year after leading some kind of demonstration, so I hired him as a civil servant with the stipulation that he had to complete his degree—something I'm proud that he did via correspondence courses. Kerr, Howick, and I worked hard to build the program up and turn it around. I had the pleasure of co-authoring a book with Howick called *Assessing Technology Transfer.* We endeavored to put the field in perspective while also exploring America's history of patent management, which is where technology and the granting of patents come together.

Thomas Jefferson was actually the first administrator of the patent office as secretary of the treasury, and he denied the first patent application he received—a process for turning salt water into drinking water—because the system was considered "old technology" well-known to most ship captains. But, in the first instance of technology transfer in the United States, Jefferson had a staff member publish a report on that patent application, ensuring that people did know it was possible to purify salt water and make it suitable for drinking.

In addition to authoring the book, I became NASA's primary spokesman on technology transfer and the economic benefits of space exploration. In this capacity, NASA sent me to a half-dozen European capital cities to speak on these topics, beyond my many speeches on the subjects domestically. I also traveled to beautiful Vienna, Austria, in 1969, near the end of my tenure, to attend a United Nation's conference on the peaceful uses of outer space. After making a speech in Paris, the head of the French space program and his wife took my wife and me on a tour of the city after a delicious dinner—and we received similar royal treatment in Rome, Berlin, The Hague, and other destinations. Officials from all these countries wanted to know about NASA and the space program. Instead of sending astronauts, who were busy with training, they sent me.

While I could talk with ease about the economic advantages of the space program, I didn't have enough time in my job to master the scientific side of space probes and unmanned flights. That occasionally caused some awkward moments. If I gave a speech about technology transfer, I'd invariably get a technical question about a particular satellite or piece of equipment. I'd have to stop the questioner and explain that I wasn't a scientist or engineer. But other than that, I fully enjoyed serving as an international ambassador of sorts for our space endeavors. And I always got the audience's attention by showing slides of technology coming through NASA—things like paint on a metal surface that could withstand a blowtorch, even after the metal had melted; or a wheelchair that could maneuver up steps or on beaches with mechanical legs, rather than wheels.

It struck me during my travels, and truly anywhere I found myself at NASA, what a long way I had come from the streets of Chambersburg—and where all those miles I'd hitchhiked as a kid had led me. I was acutely aware of that almost daily, and heard it from more than a few people. It made me feel very good.

Thinking back on this period, I only wish I had done a better job of writing papers about the value of our technology transfer mission. For example, one genius of a young man who worked for me created a retrieval system for documents. At our height, we were adding five thousand titles to the system every week in the Scientific and Technical Information Systems Division, with thousands of scientists and engineers using our library of documents. It was imperative that they all were able to locate the titles quickly, and this system was programmed to allow them to do just that. What this young man who worked for me had created was an early version of a computerized search engine.

The work he did laid the groundwork for all of the search engines in computer applications today—the precursor for an innovation we all take for granted, but one that drives education and entertainment across the globe, every second of every day. NASA, by no means, was the only organization working on search engines back then—many places were. But they all contributed to perfecting the process, and often relied on NASA's brainpower to find a solution, or ask, "How are you guys approaching this problem?" I point to this as just one illustration among thousands of the value of the space program.

Overall, if you had to pick one word to describe what I did, it would be "organizer." I organized the publications program and the computer program. I was smart enough to know what I didn't know and knew the importance of getting good people to work for me. The fact was, many talented people wanted to come to NASA during this time—we received thousands of resumes every single day. You could practically reach out and touch the electricity inside the building.

NASA had become an effort involving nearly three hundred thousand people—scientists, engineers, and some of the brightest people in the country, including some thirty thousand in government and two hundred fifty thousand in the private sector. Combined, they worked on this huge instrument that would take men to the vicinity of the moon, put two of them onto the surface, leave half the lunar liftoff vessel sitting on surface of the moon, while the other half launched with the two astronauts to rendezvous with the orbiting command capsule and then return to Earth's atmosphere without burning up. It was a terribly complicated process and thousands of people were working on their own myriad little pieces of it.

Needless to say, this was an incredibly exciting time for me, and off the charts as far as being busy. I always arrived at the office at 7:00 a.m.—one of the hallmarks of my work life—and didn't get back home until after dinner. Breene and I had a running joke about who would be at our desk first in our desire to get an early start on the day's work. I stayed on the move constantly, whether it was roaming through the office to talk to employees, being in meetings, or making frequent trips to our multiple centers around the country.

I got to know many of the astronauts in the program—they trained at the Houston Space Center, but also at Cape Kennedy, and occasionally they traveled to Washington where we saw them all at the executive dining room and had a chance to chat. I also met Wernher von Braun, the famed rocket inventor for Nazi Germany during World War II who became the leading rocket scientist for the United States after the war. He was running the operation in Huntsville, Alabama, and he and his staff often were in Washington as well, adding to the vibrant atmosphere.

It certainly helped that we enjoyed the vigorous support of President Johnson, who had been a strong backer of the space program for years—and helped pave the way for Houston's Manned Spacecraft Center, which was renamed in his honor in 1973. NASA administrator James Webb, a hard-charging and absolutely brilliant man, was a close friend of Johnson's, which also helped our cause. LBJ, in fact, was the first US president I ever met. I was introduced to him in the Rose Garden with Webb as part of a civil service awards day, honoring up-and-coming young people in federal service. The heads of all governmental agencies and departments were told by the White House to bring two bright, young, up-and-coming stars—and apparently I qualified. I don't know if I was a star, but I did know how to multitask. A young attorney and I were selected to attend the event, where Webb debated with secretary of the treasury Henry Fowler about which one of them had held the most jobs in government—until Johnson walked over, shook our hands, and thanked us for our efforts. It was a special moment I can remember vividly to this day.

As I mentioned previously, NASA had its critics and wasn't always such a rose garden of a place to work. When I arrived in 1964, the organization had experienced a series of setbacks, including six with the Ranger program. The goal of those unmanned trips to the moon was to get close-up images of the lunar surface, with the craft transmitting its photos before crashing—by design—into the surface and being destroyed.

But the missions ended twice in failures of the lunar prototype in 1961, followed by three spacecraft failures in 1962, and a camera failure in 1963. Congress actually launched an investigation into what it deemed management problems with NASA, which led to a reorganization of the agency just before Breene Kerr and I got there. Of course, there were moments to celebrate, too, such as John Glenn's successful mission on February 20, 1962, when he circled the earth four times at speeds reaching seventeen thousand miles per hour before splashing down in the Atlantic. But even Glenn quipped about the potential problems that existed when asked how it felt during the landmark launch: "How would you feel if you were strapped to a machine with ten thousand components and every one of them built by the low-cost bidder?"

In 1965, I remember sitting in a packed NASA auditorium when Ranger 8 was counting down toward its planned impact with the moon. About two hundred of us all listened to the encouraging *beep-beep-beep* sound—hoping that it would go silent when the spacecraft completed its journey, successfully transmitting photos and then crashing. When the beeps stopped—signaling the module had made impact—the entire auditorium burst into cheers and applause.

The Ranger spacecraft was so much less complex than the Apollo designs that followed, but it was still an essential part of the learning process that eventually helped complete our manned mission to the moon. Tragically, Apollo 11 followed the deaths of astronauts Gus Grissom, Ed White, and Roger Chaffee, who were poised to make the first manned mission of the US Apollo Manned Lunar Landing Program. They were to have completed a low orbital Earth test of the Apollo Command Service Module, but they never made it. During a launch rehearsal at Cape Canaveral Air Force Launch Station on January 27, 1961, they perished in a fire that engulfed the cabin.

Every one of us at NASA experienced a deep sense of shock and sadness for the losses of these great men—and for their families and friends. We all felt such a sense of family within the organization that the tragedy lingered with us for many months. At the same time, we knew that it was vital to press on with our work. And we did so, even as both houses of Congress convened committee inquiries into the accident. The investigation pointed to problems with a NASA contractor, but the committees eventually concluded that it had no connection to the accident, and the source of the fire could not be pinpointed with certainty. Nevertheless, this was a dark and difficult period for NASA—capped by a suspension of manned flights for twenty months to fix any potential problems that could lead to a similar disaster.

Considering the sensitivity of all the information we dealt with, you might assume that much of our work at NASA was highly classified. But interestingly enough, that couldn't have been further from the truth. A decision had been made by the Kennedy and Johnson administrations to keep everything unclassified. Many people felt we should have shielded the inner workings of our endeavors from public view—including von Braun, who wanted communications among astronauts in the capsule to be private. "What if the liftoff from the moon doesn't work?" he asked.

The answer from high-ranking NASA officials: the world would be allowed to hear the conversations, over open communication lines, no matter what. That kind of transparency was essential in engendering a feeling of trust with the public. I'm so proud that I could be part of what was accomplished at NASA during this memorable era. We went from the low regard much of the nation held toward NASA in the early 1960s to an organization that gave the country a positive outlook on solving problems. And I can tell you today, without hesitation, that the country got its investment in space back about one thousand times over.

We helped to make things smaller, better, and more reliable from a technological perspective. And we made things safer. I remember taking one particular piece of information that came out of the aeronautics program and peddling it to anyone who might utilize it to enhance roadway safety. I traveled to Harrisburg,

Pennsylvania, on a holiday and met with the governor and his entire staff, showing them a movie to make my point. The film demonstrated that both automobiles and airplanes hydroplaned dangerously—rising off the surface like a water skier—if you had the wrong combination of water on the asphalt, tire pressure, and the speed of the vehicle. I explained that the brakes would no longer work, causing the vehicle to skim out of control.

Hard as it might be to believe, nobody knew much about hydroplaning back then. And many people in power didn't believe it—including airline pilots. So we made films and gave presentations to educate engineers and government officials. Fast forward fifty years, and every major airport in the country has had its runways grooved to let the water dissipate, and every state in the country has grooved sections on highways to help reduce accidents. Think of how many lives may have been saved by that one little piece of knowledge developed by NASA.

Just consider some of the other ways NASA discoveries have enhanced the way we live our lives: weather satellites that also save lives—as well as billions of dollars—because people can prepare for violent storms; long-distance communications satellites that triggered a worldwide explosion in that type of technology; solar energy, stemming from work on building unmanned, solar-powered spacecraft to operate at high altitudes; artificial limbs, resulting from NASA's work with space robotics; ventricle assist devices, developed by NASA in collaboration with world renowned cardiologists to create a heart pump for patients awaiting a heart transplant, and even invisible braces so popular with teens and adults today. The material—translucent polycrystalline alumina—was invented by NASA's Advanced Ceramics Research, in conjunction with a private company to protect infrared antennae on heat-seeking missiles. I encourage you to look online for more. The list goes on and on.

There's no doubt in my mind that NASA inspired children to become better students, attracting countless youngsters to science and technology in their educational pursuits. Before NASA, you couldn't drag kids in that direction, but as we began to capture the country's imagination, enrollment in science and engineering schools increased dramatically. That's a wonderful contribution in my view. In addition, many scientists and engineers began to emigrate from Europe to continue their careers in the United States because America was where all the action was. This resulted in something of a "brain drain" of overseas expertise, much to the dismay of foreign governments.

But one of the biggest offshoots of the Apollo 11's successful mission was a surge in national confidence—a feeling that we could do anything. How many times have you heard the phrase: "We can put a man on the moon, so why can't we do this or do that." Our attitude as a country was that the sky truly *was* the limit, and that's an intangible you cannot put a price on. That's a hugely significant byproduct of NASA's contributions.

It never ceased to amaze me when I heard critics of NASA say, "Why would you spend the money on the moon?" First of all, we didn't spend money on the moon—we spent money on Earth—with all the workers who built the endless amount of equipment needed for the mission. Second, we created—as I've explained—previously unavailable technological breakthroughs that benefitted mankind in countless ways. Third, we changed America's attitude of what was possible and achievable. And finally, we planted the seeds for new generations of scientists and engineers to come. That is the lasting legacy of NASA's quest to reach the moon.

From a personal perspective, I couldn't be more gratified by two honors I received at the agency—NASA's Superior Achievement Award and the Exceptional Service Medal. In addition, I'll never forget Frank Borman's Apollo 8 mission, a precursor to Apollo 11, when he circled the moon in 1968. On Christmas Eve, Borman read from Genesis 1—"In the beginning, God created the heavens and the earth . . ."—as millions of people around the world watched and listened. My spine still tingles when I think of that.

But the greatest reward was traveling to Florida to watch the launch with my two sons and their buddy—and then watching history being made on Sunday evening, July 20, 1969. Webb had left NASA at this point, and LBJ was no longer president, so they weren't around to bask in the celebration. New administrator, Thomas Paine, and President Richard Nixon were getting all the publicity for a program that had been carried out by others, which didn't seem right to me. I remember staying home in front of my TV set and tuning in to Walter Cronkite's coverage on CBS. Like millions of Americans, I listened anxiously as Neil Armstrong deftly piloted the lunar module to the surface, while Buzz Aldrin relayed altitude and velocity data, and Collins piloted the command module. And like countless others, I cheered as Armstrong calmly uttered, "The Eagle has landed."

The next day, we watched giddily as Armstrong walked along the moon's dusty surface and uttered his famous words: "That's one small step for (a) man, one giant leap for mankind." And soon after, he and Aldrin planted the American flag in the lunar surface—an emotional sight for anyone connected with the Apollo program. When the command module Columbia splashed down safely in the Pacific Ocean three days later, it was hard to believe the mission that had begun with Kennedy's mandate eight years earlier was over—and completed in such spectacular fashion. And as a footnote, I'm proud to say that both Borman and Armstrong would one day join me as my career moved in new directions.

Against such a celebratory backdrop surrounding Apollo 11, it was tempting for me to ponder a long-term career with NASA. I could easily have stayed thirty or forty years, but I had been giving serious thought to making a change. I'd gone into NASA as a consultant and had fully expected to leave fairly quickly.

I wouldn't have traded my years there for anything and, in many ways, working for NASA built an invaluable foundation for what was to come later in my life.

I had to testify before congressional committees on numerous occasions, and became quite comfortable with what can be a nerve-wracking experience. In other instances, I sat behind James Webb when he testified—ready to provide answers on technology utilization if needed. Webb was one of the great pros of all time and it was a treat to watch him in action before congressional committees. He was a magnificent mind and speaker. Someone said of him: "Getting an answer out of Jim Webb is like trying to take a drink out of a fire hydrant." He gave you everything you could possibly want to know—and more—on a topic, and he made all of his administrators better at what we did.

I also went to Capitol Hill many times to lobby. Bear in mind, when I first arrived at NASA, the technology utilization program was the only item in our budget that congressional leaders wanted to cut! But after two years, they were adding to our budget because they realized how productive our work was. That said, I knew that I didn't want to make a career in government. A number of people I held in high regard counseled me that if that's how I felt, I shouldn't stay more than five years or it would become too difficult to make a change.

The year of the moon landing marked my fifth with NASA, so I had quietly begun looking around for the next challenge. A friend I knew from the doctoral program at Indiana was working with a systems company in suburban Maryland, and he thought I'd be the right man to run it. Saying goodbye to NASA wasn't going to be easy. I knew a lot of people would think I was absolutely crazy for walking away from a high-level position at the height of the agency's success, with the opportunity to make an entire career there. But I was convinced it was the right time to make a move—and this time my benevolent boss, Breene Kerr, wasn't going to be able to talk me out of it.

One month after the unforgettable return of Apollo 11, I was in my new job. I felt as if I'd landed well, but quickly discovered how far off the mark I was.

5 From a Big Stumble to One Giant Leap

THE NEW ORGANIZATION was called the *Systems Science Development Corporation*—hardly the glamorous, dynamic image inspired by the world-renowned acronym, NASA. But the computer company, which primarily served financial institutions, offered a sizable raise in pay from government work. And its search committee promptly zeroed in on the man—still two years shy of his fortieth birthday—who had proven his mastery of multiple systems in the space program.

The increase in money and the title of president both weighed heavily in the plus column as Dick Lesher pondered the opportunity. The timing for a new challenge felt right, and he wouldn't have to uproot his family to make the move since the firm was based in nearby Silver Spring, Maryland. So he accepted the job offer—and, in short order, came to regret it.

Systems Science Development turned out not to be well connected in the financial industry and business languished. In his eagerness to not overstay the five-year window at NASA, Lesher had taken his first professional misstep.

Rather than compound the mistake, he decided to cut his losses after several months on the job and resigned. The Indiana University friend who had recruited him left with him, and together they started a systems consulting business, *Parklow & Associates*, in North Bethesda—along the lines of the one Lesher had run briefly while teaching at Ohio State. But their attempt to gain traction in the greater Washington, DC, area was unsuccessful, and the friend soon left to form his own company.

This was definitely not what Lesher had envisioned when he planned on parlaying his stellar career at NASA into a new career. Now on his own as a struggling consultant, he needed a break. That's when former NASA administrator James E. Webb called Lesher and asked if he would consider taking on a company, International Telecommunications Network. Several of Webb's friends had invested in ITN and it was performing poorly.

Knowing Lesher's track record for getting things done quickly and well, Webb said, "Dick, would you go in there and take a look at this thing and see if you can straighten it out?" If Lesher could turn it around, perhaps that would change his fortunes for the better.

He agreed. But ITN's problems persisted and soon there was another issue: the company was unable to make payments. And it was only a matter of time before Lesher's consulting firm couldn't pay its own bills and was forced to close the doors.

It was the low point of Lesher's life—the mirror opposite of elation he'd felt from the moon landing. It was the first time he hadn't succeeded at whatever he'd set out to achieve, leaving him feeling deflated and unsure of his next move. His company was insolvent, his partners had vanished, and he was left to pay a substantial bill to the Internal Revenue Service without the benefit of a job.

But what sustained him in this dark hour was the knowledge that he'd been down before—with memories of being evicted with his family from their apartment for failure to pay the rent, surviving the unpredictable tirades and beatings of his father, and learning to rely on his own wits and work ethic to get by.

The strengths he developed as a child kept him moving forward now—straight into a new opportunity that changed everything.

It's fair to say I went straight from frustration and failure right to garbage—and I couldn't have been happier.

In the midst of searching for a solution to my mounting woes, I was talking on the phone one day and someone happened to mention a job opening with the National Center for Solid Waste Disposal. I can't remember who brought it up, and I have to admit that the name didn't do much for me, either. But the position itself certainly sounded promising—a high-paying executive role rubbing shoulders with a blue-ribbon board of directors and CEOs from some of America's largest corporations. "How can I put my name in the hat for that?" I wondered.

Some quick research made me even more interested. Top executives from twelve industries, responding to the urging from the Nixon administration, had established the National Center for Solid Waste Disposal in the fall of 1969 amid mounting clamor and concerns about pollution. The Environmental Protection Agency had already been created, leading to a sharper focus on clean air and clean water, and new regulations were implemented to maintain those high standards.

Solid waste was considered the so-called third pollution at a time when there was virtual *hysteria* in the country over one environmental problem or another. And in this volatile atmosphere, companies that used consumer packaging—especially containers—were worried that Congress might pass a new legislation that would seriously hamper them. They grew increasingly concerned that certain kinds of packaging would be outlawed or taxed or that all bottles and cans would require a deposit and have to be returned to the store—completely disrupting the entire distribution system, since delivery trucks weren't properly equipped for hauling garbage back on a return trip. In addition, companies didn't want to take any chances that new laws might create restrictions on what materials they could use. They were afraid, for instance, that plastics or Styrofoam would be banned. The truth was, many of the solutions being proposed were outlandish and wrong-headed.

As a result, against this wave of hysteria, leadership at these twelve industries—along with some of their labor unions—decided to be proactive and form a company to do battle on the issue of solid-waste disposal. They set up the National Center for Solid Waste Disposal as a way of creating their own organization and policies for dealing with solid waste materials. The challenge was that municipalities were running out of landfill space to dispose of solid waste. The new center wanted to develop a systems approach to solving that problem—one that dealt effectively with refuse disposal while also recovering resources that could be re-used by industry. And they were absolutely committed to the entire process.

Two CEOs from each of the industries comprised the board of directors and included companies such as Anheuser-Busch, Coors Brewing, Coca Cola, Reynolds Metals, Kroger, Monsanto, Alcoa, US Steel, General Foods, Proctor & Gamble, and Giant grocery stores. In addition, two trade unions were also on the board, and the legendary Donald Kendall, longtime chief executive officer of Pepsico, was elected chairman.

Kendall was larger than life. One of his many grandiose moves was to barter an arrangement with the Soviet Union in less-than-cordial times. He wanted to distribute Pepsi to the Soviets, but they didn't have the money to import the soft drink. So the two parties worked out a novel deal: Soviet officials allowed Kendall to sell Pepsi there if he agreed to take an equal amount of Stolichnaya vodka in return. He gladly did, acquiring a company to retail the vodka in the United States. That's just one example of what a great businessman he was, and why I was delighted that he was chairing the organization. Kendall was also regarded as a great access point to the Nixon administration because he was close to the president. He had even employed Nixon as a counsel to Pepsi during the brief period he was not in government.

I knew this was the opportunity I was waiting for. My old competitive fire began to burn—and I immediately went to work calling any well-placed friends I could think of. They, in turn, reached out to their connections, all with the aim of bringing my name to the attention of the search agency assembling candidates. Eventually, through all my networking, several people contacted the search committee members on my behalf and told them that I was their guy. That led to a series of interviews, and everyone I spoke with seemed to like the idea of a guy with a space systems background. Or maybe America's industry heads just needed somebody dumb enough to take on and figure out the garbage problem—and that was me.

Years later, I learned in a letter written by Kendall that more than eight hundred candidates were interviewed for the job—in a highly competitive selection process—before I was chosen. I'll get back to that pivotal letter later in this chapter. At the time, all I knew was that I was elated to be offered the job as president and CEO of the center in 1971—ending a period of deep uncertainty and vaulting me into a brand new adventure. August Busch III and the US Brewers Association were the primary movers and shakers behind the effort, and I remember having breakfast with him soon after I was hired. He said, "Dick, can you fix this?" I responded, "Well, you want me to do it with smoke and mirrors, and that takes longer because you didn't give me a big enough budget to tackle a national problem."

Nevertheless, I couldn't wait to get started helping shape the organization's direction. I already had one idea. At the very first board meeting, I recommended that we change the name from the National Center for Solid Waste Disposal to the National Center for Resource Recovery. It had a much more engaging ring to it—the beauty of it was that it focused on the *right* solution instead of disposal. "Resource Recovery" was where we wanted to place the emphasis: a mechanized approach to processing garbage and pulling out whatever substances we could of value, thereby focusing on recovering beneficial material from the waste stream. And they wanted a NASA systems approach to drive the entire process.

I put together a great team. We immersed ourselves in everything written on the topic—and we went to work studying what was working, what was not, and what might work. Our over-arching intent was to demonstrate that we didn't need to worry about running out of land for landfills, and promote landfills that were being re-purposed—such as in Los Angeles, where they were filling in canyons and building golf courses and parks on top.

In many respects, the work tapped my previous experience at NASA, which was all about systems and information flow. We conducted two demonstrations—one in Washington, DC, and another in New Orleans, which had a unique solid waste problem since their water table was only a few inches below the ground: if they dug a hole for disposal, there was a good chance they'd hit that water. Because they couldn't bury garbage in a landfill, they had no choice but to incinerate it. That's where we entered the picture, helping to develop a system that removed the non-burning waste and working closely with city officials to implement the approach.

The key to making the refuse more burnable was to process it. When it comes off a municipal waste-hauling truck, it's all mixed together—with about 55 percent of the load paper and plastic, and the remaining 45 percent inert material such as aluminum, steel, and glass. The trick was removing those resources, some of which could be recycled. With that in mind, we devised a system that consisted of conveyer belts and magnets that pulled out the steel, filters that got rid of stones and glass, with blowers that pushed the plastic, paper, and food waste to an area where it could be dealt with—that type of approach. The paper, plastic, and food remnants burned easily in incinerators, creating a viable source of fuel and energy that could be utilized for powering equipment on the site. That's an example of the type of work we undertook going forward, addressing both solid waste disposal and resource recovery. At the time, I could *never* have imagined a scenario that occurred recently in Germany, where six energy recovery units ran out of garbage and had to actually import garbage from the United Kingdom— simply to generate power at their sites!

With an approved budget of two million in 1972, our center set out on similar missions nationwide to mechanically separate potential resources from refuse, separating the organic from the non-organic. My staff included four or five highly capable former colleagues from NASA, a handful of PhDs with science and engineering backgrounds from other organizations—all very bright people up to the challenge. And we persuaded a lot of people that we had a solution, including government officials tasked with addressing the issue. To spread our message, we created and distributed a good number of publications on the topic and outfitted a traveling van that our experts drove to cities across the country.

At each stop, they would make appearances to city leaders, explaining the value of resource recovery, incorporating posters and photographs, explaining what material got recycled and what did not, educating people on the issue as best we could—and trying to diffuse the public concern so some irrational policy wasn't enacted. Believe me, there were some wild ideas floating around, such as the one suggested to me by the Council on Environmental Quality. The agency, an arm of the White House, was run by Russell E. Train. And believe it or not, someone from his ranks was ready to go through with a proposal to outlaw all the classified advertising supplements newspapers included in their Sunday sections. The staffer, a young woman, told me, "Well, I don't use them—most people don't look at the classified sections, so all they're doing is filling up the landfills. That's why we should do away with them."

I said, "Do you know what country you're living in? Do you understand anything of the economics of the newspaper industry? You'd put newspapers out of business—classifieds are one of the things that keeps them *in* business!" She replied, much to my astonishment, "I hadn't thought about that, but maybe we should tell the newspapers they can only publish classified sections once a month."

I couldn't believe what I was hearing, and responded without any attempt to mask my bewilderment. "You know, if you go forward with any of those crazy ideas, not only will you get fired but your boss will, too!" As a side note, I later stumbled upon some memos from my board members who wanted Nixon to fire Train and hire me in that job—but nobody ever talked to me about it and I wouldn't have been interested anyway.

In any event, the idea of doing away with classified advertising was just one more example of the insanity being advocated back then by some zealots, many of whom were angry that we would be so bold as to call ourselves the "National Center"—as if we were claiming to be the world champions before playing a game. But we knew what we were doing and, gradually, people began to listen.

As I mentioned, part of our educational initiatives involved landfills. Areas with organic garbage buried in the earth produced methane gas that had to be released from the ground. This was strikingly illustrated in a trip I made to Japan during this time, when I saw one of the largest landfills in the world, located on the edge of Tokyo Bay. Japan was a nation importing 98 percent of its fossil fuel—even though its massive landfill was venting off methane gas into the atmosphere via pipes coming out of the ground, simply wasting it rather than capturing it and utilizing it as an on-site energy source.

I showed pictures of this to my board when I returned and said, "Here's a country that has to import nearly all of its fuel, yet it's venting off precious methane into the atmosphere!" After that trip, we began actively advocating capturing methane at landfills around the United States. We received tremendous pushback in spite of the evidence we presented about the benefits of this system. Garbage companies didn't want anything to do with this, convinced it would drive up their costs. But today, almost all of them in the country have adopted our way of thinking—capturing the methane at the site of the landfills to at least power the equipment there and other sites nearby. There's no question that we were ahead of the curve on this. At the time, it was considered a groundbreaking solution. And, in fact, methane capturing is employed today in various parts of the world.

Ironically, all the emphasis placed on returning soda and beer bottles to the store as part of the recycling movement actually *contributed* to the pollution problem. Now you had dirty bottles that sat in the back of the store until they were picked up. The bottles attracted cockroaches, requiring store managers to spray chemicals to keep away the pests—and creating a negative chain-reaction from putting soiled containers back into the food chain. It made no sense! The bottom line was that returnable bottles resulted in a waste of time and manpower and was never a good idea in my book.

Our efforts were successful enough to prompt astronaut Neil Armstrong to join our distinguished board of directors. His presence enhanced the visibility of our work—everyone, it seemed, wanted to rub shoulders with the man who walked on the moon, and that opened more doors for us around the country as I gave numerous talks, stressing the importance of resource recovery. As a side note, I'd developed a friendship with John Glenn during my years at NASA and his daughter eventually came to work for me at NCRR, joining my other hires from the agency.

I'd joke to people that the glass of water they just had might have been served at the Last Supper, pointing out that the water in our global system continues to circulate. Or I'd quip that the gold in the watch on someone's wrist might have been mined by the ancient Egyptians, because gold throughout the centuries is often recycled and turned into new products. I felt entirely fulfilled by our work and proud of what we were accomplishing. In the end, we achieved something that I regard as monumental: eliminating the hysteria and replacing it with a common-sense, mechanical approach. In only a few years, we changed attitudes worldwide, shifting the mission from disposal to recovery. And while we haven't had a national solution yet, we're moving toward one in a much more systematic and intelligent fashion—a huge accomplishment for a relatively small organization.

I fully planned to stick with the job. But quite unexpectedly in 1975, during my fifth year, I received a phone call from a friend who told me that the president of the United States Chamber of Commerce was retiring soon—and that my name had been mentioned as a possible candidate. The Chamber was not an organization I'd given much thought to or had any dealings with, but there didn't seem to be any harm in trying to learn more about the opening. I spoke to someone on the search committee, saying, "Look, I really don't want to pursue this any further unless there's a good chance of succeeding. I work for an excellent organization, with an excellent board, and I don't want to mess things up."

I was assured that I would at least be a finalist, and that was enough incentive to take the next step. The first thing I did was talk to Kendall, who wasn't sure this would be a good move for me. "Dick, you know the Chamber is just a big, dormant organization—it's an important institution, but it hasn't been for the last twenty years. Do you think you could help turn it around?"

"I'm sure I could," I replied. "But you'd have to help. You'd have to come over there and serve on my board—and we'd have to bring some of the National Center board members over as well." My reasoning was that the US Chamber had a history of having people you'd never heard of on its board—vice presidents who couldn't speak for their own companies, let alone their industry.

Kendall thought I had a point, and felt I should pursue the position quietly—without letting the Chamber's search committee contact anybody from my current board of directors for reference purposes. "If they want to talk to somebody with the Center, I'll tell them I represent the board of directors and they can talk to me," he explained. "If it comes down to you being a finalist, then they can talk to anybody they want."

That sounded like a good plan. And the more I looked into the opportunity, the more I wanted to compete for it. The job obviously would fulfill my desire to take on a big challenge—and would be highly satisfying if I succeeded.

Kendall and I had worked closely together with the National Center for Resource Recovery, and had even sat down at one point with President Nixon to give him a detailed report of all we were accomplishing. I knew that Kendall didn't want me to leave, but he saw an upside if I got the job. "The US Chamber has a lot more potential of doing good for American business if you can turn it around and make it into something effective," he remarked.

With that, Kendall proceeded to write a strong letter of recommendation on my behalf to the search firm, Hay Associates. To this day, his words are a source of enormous pride and gratitude. Here is an excerpt:

> In my opinion, the US Chamber of Commerce is one of the most important institutions in this country. The challenges facing the Chamber are now greater than ever, and it is extremely important that the right man be selected to fill that position. It is only because I feel so strongly about the Chamber that I would consider incurring the great loss we would have if Dick left.
>
> The individual chosen must be unique and outstanding. He must have top-level government experience in the executive branch, coupled with intimate knowledge of the legislative branch. I would think it would be ideal if he had both line and staff management experience in both large and small organizations; if he had a vast experience in public speaking, including radio, television, and international exposure; if he had the highest order of judgment, creativity, and perhaps, most importantly, if his academic and professional backgrounds were very heavy in finance and economics, systems management, and communications with all media.
>
> A man who combines all of this is truly unique, but that's what we set out to find four years ago, and that's what we found in Dr. Lesher. His performance in all of these areas has been truly remarkable. The firm that conducted the search for the first president of the National Center for Resource Recovery carefully screened through 830 top executives from business and government, before recommending Dick as their top choice.

The individual who had run the Chamber previously, Arch Booth, was known to be stodgy and set in his ways. The organization was viewed in the same manner—old school, unimaginative, and not an exciting force on the business landscape. I was confident I could bring needed energy and change to the organization and worked my way through the lengthy interview process. There were so many questions I had no way to prepare for, other than having prepared for this kind of test my whole life.

There are twenty-five hundred state and local chambers and many of those executives aspired to this job, along with top officials from trade associations and corporate presidents all actively pursuing the position—a highly appealing one in visibility and compensation. The initial pool of several hundred applicants was gradually whittled down to a handful of finalists, and—as promised—I was one of them. I eventually sat down with the entire executive committee. Each member interviewed me, one after the next, at the Metropolitan Club in downtown Washington, DC. Early on in the process, I remember quipping to members of the selection committee, "I'm really flattered that you have time to talk to a garbage man." I think that won some of them over, but it still felt like my doctoral days when I was defending my dissertation to the committee.

At one point during the interview, I was asked a probing question that might have been a turning point: What would I do if the board came down with policy positions opposite to what I believed? I thought for a moment and answered honestly: "First of all, I'd be surprised if that happens, but if it does in an isolated incident, then of course I'm going to honor the policy. But I need to add that if is this happened very often, I would probably leave because it would mean I was in the wrong place. It would mean the Chamber, in my view, would be doing the wrong things. I expect the organization to produce conservative principles that honor the opposition to government growth, spending, and taxes. And if we came out on the opposite side of those issues very often, it's the wrong place for me."

I believe my straightforward reply made a positive impact on the search committee, as did my comment about the integrity of the policy-making process. I underscored that the Chamber board is the body that sets policy. I could influence it, as could any other board member, but once the vote is taken, that's the position that must be honored. Making this point was reassuring to my interviewers—and, ironically, would one day surface as the central issue in my moment of truth with the Chamber, rooted in an unforeseen and serious conflict with the White House. But more on that later. There were still countless more questions for me to answer—and I even underwent psychological testing as part of the search process. Finally, I received a phone call from the head of the search firm at Hay Associates—he offered me the job, and I couldn't have been happier.

I knew one of my first challenges was to try and change the attitude not just about the US Chamber of Commerce, but also about American business in general. Business's image had been getting beat up in the media during the past decade, viewed more as a necessary evil than a needed catalyst for growth. The mood of the country had soured during the Vietnam War, followed by Watergate, and the eventual resignation of President Nixon in 1974. A widespread sentiment of mistrust of the establishment had taken root, and business—or how many people viewed it as a whole—was a casualty.

To counteract that, members of the Chamber's board wanted a more vigorous, positive presence representing American business, and they felt I was the man for the job. I took over on April 29, 1975, with high hopes but no idea of the ride I was about to begin. All I knew was that my predecessor wouldn't allow me in the Chamber of Commerce building until my first day at work. I believe he wanted me to fall on my face and then be asked to come out of retirement to resume his duties.

The Chamber wrote and distributed a *Voice of Business* column at the time that was sent out to several hundred newspapers around the country. He tried to take the concept and name with him when he left, but I said, "No way! That doesn't belong to him—it belongs to the Chamber." Then he wanted an office in the building and I said, "No. If he needs space to go through his mail, we can rent him a little space next door." The next thing he wanted was for me to hire his secretary, and I said, "No thanks, my secretary is coming with me."

Soon after dealing with that awkward changing of the guard, I encountered some pushback from various Chamber of Commerce executives around the country, because I didn't have a background as a Chamber executive myself—yet here I was running the national organization. But after a few months on the job, some of the leaders who had expressed reservations about me changed their minds and silenced the others. The head of the San Francisco Chamber, in fact, sent out word to membership that I was the right man to run the US Chamber at this stage in its history and that the naysayers should back off.

That was a turning point in terms of my widespread acceptance. And it made life a little easier, because it was time to engineer significant changes in the way we did business—powered by the mission-driven approach I'd learned at NASA, practiced at NCRR, and was now ready to put into action with the US Chamber of Commerce.

6   A Better Way of Doing Business

On a sunny Washington, DC, morning, a crowd of onlookers amassed on the sidewalk along Pennsylvania Avenue, standing outside the entrance of the Willard Hotel. The respectful refrain of "Good morning, Mr. President," rippled through the throng of bystanders as the nation's twenty-seventh chief executive, William Howard Taft, stepped out of a large White House limousine. He smiled and waved at the group and then strode inside the hotel lobby.

The date was April 22, 1912, and some seven hundred delegates waited inside for a first-ever national conference of commercial and trade organizations. The purpose was to establish a single organization that would represent the many disparate business groups and associations in the country at that time. Taft proposed the idea to Congress in December 1911 and, in March, directed Secretary of Labor and Commerce Charles Nagel to formally arrange the gathering. The turnout was remarkable—with delegates coming from every state in the country, as well as Alaska, the Philippines, Puerto Rico, and the American Chambers of Commerce of Paris, Brussels, and Constantinople.

The attendees inside the Willard's large conference room burst into spontaneous applause at the sight of Taft. He spoke briefly, but long enough to urge the delegates to create a new national body of businessmen. "We want your assistance," he declared, "in carrying on the government in reference to those matters that affect the business and business welfare of the country, and we do not wish to limit your discretion in that matter." One day later, the US Chamber of Commerce was born—with the development trumpeted in the next day's Washington Post:

> *BUSINESS PUT THROUGH IN FORTY-EIGHT HOURS—GOVERNMENT WILL RECEIVE POWERFUL AID IN SOLVING HARASSING COMMERCIAL PROBLEMS—BODY FORMED AT THE SOLICITATION OF PRESIDENT TAFT AND NAGEL.*

Now, sixty-three years later, a new man, with a new vision, was at the helm. And the organization rooted in the nation's past was about to be propelled into the future.

Before I began formulating initiatives intended to kick-start the Chamber of Commerce into a modern, relevant force, I had taken time to immerse myself in the organization's past. Like many Americans, I honestly knew precious little about the institution beyond its name and general orientation as a proponent of business interests and opportunities. I've always been an avid reader, so I made time to acquaint myself with the history of the Chamber and the pressing issues it faced.

Beyond soaking up key facts and work of the Chamber over the decades, I focused in particular on a transformative 1971 document called the Powell Memorandum. Lewis Powell was a Richmond, Virginia, attorney eventually appointed to the US Supreme Court. Amid the increasingly hostile climate toward private enterprise, Powell had grown concerned about the state of American economic freedom. Hyperinflation loomed amid the gasoline crisis, forcing drivers to wait for hours at the gas pump in 1973. Public activism surrounding consumer and environmental issues increased, while confidence in business declined—particularly among young people and on America's college campuses. The profile of the US Chamber had diminished to such a degree that an audible voice for business no longer existed.

The situation created the backdrop for Powell's formative essay—prompted when a neighbor who served on the US Chamber Board spoke to him about the dire state of affairs for American business. Powell told the board member: "Business no longer does anything—look at how strong the opposition is; look at the attention consumer activist Ralph Nader gets." That prompted the Chamber official to ask Powell if he would write down his thoughts so he could present them to the full board. Powell gladly obliged and produced a memorandum—highlighted years later in a Chamber report produced on my watch entitled *The Spirit of Enterprise*—that quickly gained national attention. Its central thrust was as direct as it was foreboding: "business and the enterprise system are in deep trouble, and the hour is late."

Powell's memorandum forcefully advocated for increased political action across the spectrum or, as the Spirit of Enterprise phrased it, "a competitive response in the nation's courts, and an aggressive communications program on behalf of private enterprise." His unmistakable message was that the Chamber had to become active in the public eye—particularly in the fast-evolving, far-reaching medium of television, as well as the judicial system—representing American business interests before the courts and regulatory agencies. My predecessor hadn't been doing any of that, which is one of the reasons the Chamber Board hastened him out the door and brought me on board to turn the page.

When I arrived in 1975, I hadn't heard much about the Powell Memorandum. Though it had been extremely well received by the board members several years earlier, the doctrine languished amid business-as-usual routines for the antiquated organization. But after settling into my role, I took a close look at Powell's work and was extremely impressed with its ambitious scope—and sensible remedies to reinvigorate the Chamber. It was only a matter of time before I began implementing its multi-faceted mission. The challenge was to find the most effective way to put Powell's thoughts into meaningful action, reflective of my own vision for change and desire to move forward as rapidly as possible.

Bear in mind, the major overhauls I planned to engineer would have to take place with a less-than-cordial relationship with the White House. I overlapped the business-friendly administration of President Gerald Ford for only eighteen months before Georgia Governor Jimmy Carter defeated Ford in 1976, putting a Democrat back in the White House for the first time in eight years. We knew a difficult era for American business was suddenly upon us.

After Carter was elected, we brought a businessman up from Georgia who'd been involved in the Chamber movement to offer us some insights into the new president. He insisted on holding a closed-door meeting with my staff and myself, with no media allowed. And he proceeded to lay out his perspective, chapter and verse. In a peanut shell, so to speak, the peanut farmer from Plains was definitely no friend to small business or business interests in general.

For starters, our contact predicted, Carter would alienate the Congress in the first year and have a bumpy relationship with the legislative branch from then on. He proceeded to make clear that—based on Carter's tense dealings with the business community in Georgia—he would not get along with the US Chamber in any way whatsoever. Even with such a bleak portrait of what lay ahead, I held out hope that Carter and I could forge a productive relationship of some kind. But I was dead wrong and, unfortunately, our business contact from Georgia was right on the money.

The first time I ever met Carter was in a receiving line sometime in 1977 at a White House function. I began to introduce myself. He replied brusquely before I could get all the words out of my mouth, "I know who you are. The Chamber." He turned to his wife, First Lady Rosalyn Carter, and said tersely, "This is Mr. Lesher from the Chamber of Commerce." If a stare could kill, I would have been dead on the spot—her glare made it clear that I was not considered a friend of the Carters. That simply confirmed what we had been warned about: the president was anti-business, no matter how much he tried to cover it up as the small-business peanut producer. As a side note, the irony is that his brother, Billy Carter—widely portrayed as a bumbling country bumpkin—was the real businessman of the family. When our Chamber magazine profiled Billy during the Carter years, we learned that he actually had a sharp mind and agreed with many of our major policies. But to this day, history has cast him as something of a stooge. That's an injustice to Billy, who was well read, an expert on literary great Henry David Thoreau, and a man who told our writer that he never talked up his intellectual pursuits for fear of not fitting in back home.

My experiences working with the Carter administration rapidly went from cool to frosty as I lay the groundwork for change within the Chamber, speaking up loudly on behalf of business, and frequently challenging Carter's policies. In one instance, a member of his staff tried to teach me a lesson by freezing me out of a briefing at the White House. Carter was scheduled to meet with leaders of various business organizations and trade associations at a round-table session. We received an invitation for our chairman and vice chairman to join the group and, at the appointed time, the two men traveled the short distance from the Chamber office to the White House to take part. Upon their arrival, a White House staffer approached them to say, "You may wonder why the chiefs of staff of all these organizations are here, along with all these other executives, but Dick Lesher isn't part of this. Well, the reason is that Lesher is too damn hard on the President." The clear intention was to get me to back off Carter, in order to be included in future meetings of this sort.

I learned about all of this when my chairman and vice chair returned, eager to inform me of the Carter staff's ploy. "What are you going to do about this?" one of them asked me. I was miffed, to be sure, but far from rattled. "Don't worry about it," I said. "I'll fix it." The man who delivered the message to my bosses was named S. Stephen Selig III, Carter's associate for public liaison. I made an appointment with him and went to see him in the Old Executive Office Building. Not surprisingly—at least to me—he kept me waiting in the outer office before finally signaling to his secretary to bring me in.

Selig was sitting with his back to the door and took his time swinging around to face me. He reached down and picked up a cigar, chopped off the end, and lit it. Then—after all that show—Selig looked at me and remarked in a less-than-friendly tone: "Well, what can I do for you, Lesher?"

"Steve," I began, staring him right in the eyes. "We have a problem."

"We don't have a problem," he cut me off. "*You* have a problem!" With that, he shoved his cigar in my direction to underscore his displeasure.

I'd faced far more intimidating looks from my father than this bloviating, hanger-on. "Now *you* listen and listen carefully," I replied in a firm, though unmistakably angry voice. "I can have a headline on the front page of the *Washington Post* tomorrow morning saying that the Carter administration has blacklisted the president of the largest business organization in America. Now Steve, do you want to be responsible for that?"

I thought he was going to fall out of his seat.

The end result was that Selig backpedaled and changed his entire tone. And he agreed to arrange a meeting for me with his boss, Stuart Eisenstat, Carter's chief domestic policy advisor, to clear the air. I told Stu what had taken place and he told me: "Dick, that will never happen again. We won't always agree with the Chamber, but we will always show you respect. We understand why you have the positions you have, and you can rest assured nothing like this will ever happen again."

I encountered other rough patches in my dealings with the establishment—beyond the executive branch—in those early years. On one of the first trips I made to Capitol Hill, I clashed with a senior democrat from Florida who served as a committee chairman, Paul Rogers. He was displeased with a position that the Chamber had published about some issue on this or that. Furthermore, I was told that he had blustered something to the effect of, "I demand that the new Chamber president come up here and talk to me face-to-face!"

That was fine with me—I was glad to have an opportunity to state our position in person. I brought along several of my staff members and listened politely while the congressman ranted about whatever pro-business opinion we'd voiced. When he was finished, I gave it right back, meeting force with force. "I'm sorry you feel the way you do," I said, "but this is our process and, the fact is, we believe you're wrong and we're right." The lawmaker looked at me in disbelief, stunned that he had been challenged, grumbling that we hadn't heard the last about the matter.

As we left the building, my two aides grinned. "Wow," one of them said. "Our old boss would have said, 'Yes sir, Mr. Congressman, I'll do whatever you say.' And he'd have gone back to the Chamber and chewed out the staff guy who was responsible for us getting called up there in the first place."

In one instance, the difficulty I encountered had nothing to do with Carter's White House or pushy congressional figures, but within my own ranks at the Chamber. Near the end of Carter's tenure in office, we were working with his administration on a particular issue and he summoned our Chairman, Bill Verity, the head of Armco Steel and a big name in Republican political circles who went on to serve as secretary of commerce under President Reagan. Carter wanted to enlist the Chamber's support for a White House anti-inflation imitative with the acronym WIN, standing for Whip Inflation Now.

Verity came back from a lunch with Carter, stepped into my office, and informed me that we were going to have to put out a press release supporting the president. I knew that the issue ran counter to the policy of the Chamber's board of directors so I replied bluntly, "Bill, we can't do that." He bristled, insisting that I send out the release expressing our support, whereupon I responded: "You don't set the policy and I don't set the policy. The board sets the policy and currently the board is opposed to it." Verity had to back down and I moved on with a multitude of other Chamber efforts—never imagining that a very similar set of circumstances would arise in less than two years and nearly cost me my job in a far more intense showdown with a new administration.

If nothing else, my encounter with Verity was evidence of the belief I'd laid out in my job interview: that my responsibility was to adhere to the policy of the board of directors. If the search committee that hired me suspected I wouldn't run from a fight, they were right. But that's what it took as I—and, by extension, the Chamber—began to establish credibility. One of the key initiatives I put into place—signaling a new way of doing business—was the Nonpartisan Endorsement Program to support the election of pro-business candidates to Congress. This was inspired by Powell's call for intensified political action. And it eventually evolved—a decade later—into our practice of keeping a scorecard of how members of the House and Senate voted.

We made certain that everybody knew of this practice. Our purpose was to be able to identify, with pinpoint accuracy, pro-business candidates when they came up for reelection. Any legislator who voted with us 70 percent of the time or more received what I named the Spirit of Enterprise Award. But more important, the award-winners received our endorsement for reelection. That was an example of how I changed the Chamber's game to hardball on Washington's political playing field—and the tactic didn't sit well with politicians not accustomed to our more aggressive style.

I told my staff that every member of the House was going to meet with at least one member of the Chamber during the year, whether the members wanted to or not. I volunteered to meet with the tough ones—and the description certainly applied, on one memorable visit in late 1980s, to Democratic US Representative Jim Wright, the powerful Speaker of the House from Texas. When I called on Wright one day, the sparks quickly began to fly. Moments after sitting down in his office, explaining I just wanted to talk about the issues and how we could work together constructively, he snapped at me: "Mr. Lesher, I *don't like* your political action committee."

"Well, we try to be non-partisan," I interjected. "We do support some Democrats. But we base it all on our scorecard."

At that, Wright virtually jumped out of his seat with the nastiest of looks. Then he walked briskly to his door, as if he intended to throw me out of his office, and yelled: "Don't you come into my office and piss on my shoes and tell me it's raining outside!"

Obviously, the Speaker didn't buy my statement that we attempted to be non-partisan, as he continued his tirade. "All you endorse are Republicans!" I proceeded to give him the names of several Democrats we had indeed supported due to their 70 percent or higher score—though they were the more conservative Blue Dogs from the South and Southwest. Perhaps because I stayed calm in the face of his fury, Wright didn't throw me out of his office and sat back down at his desk. We wound up having a tense, yet mildly constructive, conversation—and, amazingly, we seemed to develop a foundation of mutual respect for one another, in spite of our differences. Whenever I'd see him after that, he was always friendly. It was all part of letting people know I was running a different kind of organization, and—with the help of our scorecards—the political world was catching on fast.

In the same vein as my heated sit-down with Wright, I met with another high-profile adversary, labor leader George Meany, the hard-nosed head of the American Federation of Labor and the Congress of Industrial Organizations—better known as the AFL-CIO. I called Meany up and invited him to have lunch at the plush Hay-Adams Hotel, equidistant between our respective offices near Lafayette Square. We sat down at our table and after a few pleasantries I said, "You know and I know that there are many things we'll never agree on—until hell freezes over. But there are some things that we do agree on and that we're both getting kicked in the ass on. We ought to work together on those things." Meany, who was such a legend in the union movement, listened quietly, then leaned across the table and said, "Young man, that's the speech I was gonna make to you!"

After that, the ice was broken and we had a wonderful time, trading stories and growing comfortable with one another. I told him how my father had been a union organizer in the Local 385 of the AFL-CIO—the plasterers and cement finishers. "That's where I started!" he burst out. "How did you wind up in the Chamber if your dad was a union guy?" At the end of a very enjoyable lunch, we decided we'd get together once in a while—though neither his staff nor my staff liked that idea, so not much more came from the meeting. But as far as I was concerned, it was worth the effort to spread the word of the Chamber's new, higher-profile style—whether people liked us or not.

During the Carter years, our increasing influence was particularly visible with an all-out battle with the White House over Consumer Protection Agency legislation, which was narrowly defeated by the House thanks in part to our lobbying. We began pressuring particular committee members who might be on the fence by going to their hometown, generating thousands of letters and phone calls directed at that member's office, and getting them to change or reconsider their vote.

We did the same thing when it came to labor-law reform—something the unions wanted very badly in order to make it easier to force workers to join their ranks, in the face of declining membership. We flatly opposed this as a bad idea for business, mobilized our forces to defeat the measure, and won. We had cases in which members of Congress would contact us and say, "Hey, call off the dogs! We can't get anything else done with all the mail and phone calls. I've changed my vote." This proved to be a valuable training ground for me—and the Chamber—as we continued to flex our muscles in the Reagan, Bush, and Clinton administrations.

One offshoot of all my outreach during the Carter years was that the press began paying more attention to us, and that proved to be a crucial step in our development. If any kind of business or economic issue popped up, the Chamber would be one of the first places reporters would call for a comment. I got into various battles with members of the Carter administration during this time, on one occasion taking issue with a speech made by Secretary of the Treasury, Bill Miller. In my view, his facts were entirely wrong in stating that the economy was entirely in the tank when Carter took office. My response was to hold a press conference in the Chamber building and correct Miller's erroneous view. The press corps ate it up.

I learned soon enough that the media loved that type of confrontational stance. I repeated the maneuver when consumer advisor Esther Peterson, a member of Carter's staff, made some comment that rubbed me the wrong way. So I called a press conference to point out why she was incorrect. Peterson, who'd been on my board at the National Center for Resource Recovery, came back at me hard, accusing me of being off base. I had no problem with that, because I'd managed to generate headlines, getting the Chamber's perspective out to the world. If it took holding press conferences from then on to raise our profile, I was game.

There were certainly some lighter moments in the mix of events. Every year, for instance, we went out on the town with the Committee of 100—a group of association executives, people who controlled convention spending. As a result, whenever we went out with them, we always got the red-carpet treatment because these execs represented millions of dollars of convention spending—and that meant some exquisite dinners at some of the nation's finest restaurants.

Then there was the time actor Paul Newman came to lunch at the White House. Anne Wexler, Carter's Assistant for External Affairs, was supposed to come over to the Chamber that same day for a briefing and called me that morning to ask, "Can we move the lunch over here to the White House mess? I have a good friend coming in from out of town and I promised him that if he was ever in the area, I'd show him the White House. His name is Paul Newman." I laughed—as if Anne didn't think I'd know who he was—and informed her that I'd be glad to make the change, even though I knew our banquet manager would be upset because he'd prepared a nice menu for her visit. In any event, when lunch hour neared, I headed over to the White House several minutes away and stepped into the reception room in the East Wing.

Minutes later, Newman and his famous baby blue eyes lit up the room. And almost on cue, secretaries holding notepads flooded in, wanting autographs from the box-office star, coming off big hits like *Butch Cassidy and the Sundance Kid* and *The Sting*. Soon enough, Anne's husband arrived, and the four of us—the Wexlers, Newman, and yours truly—sat in the dining room for two hours. And Newman was spectacular. He never bragged about himself, but if you asked him a question, he provided a fascinating answer. He also wanted to know about the White House and the Chamber, and what my job was like. I was so impressed with him as a person—so different than what you hear about most Hollywood superstars.

Without question, however, the most memorable time of the Carter administration took place when world events put the Chamber on center stage in 1977. As I described earlier in these pages, Egyptian President Anwar Sadat and Israeli Prime Minister Menachem Begin arrived in Washington, DC, to sign the Egypt-Israel Peace Treaty, with my organization hosting a dinner for Sadat at Chamber of Commerce headquarters in Washington, and a luncheon for Begin one day later in New York City. I will only add here that to find myself in the middle of this historic moment—so early in my tenure at the Chamber and with the eyes of the world on us—was an experience I will always treasure. At the time, I was so immersed in the fast-paced flow of events that my sole focus was in ensuring the Chamber's participation was a success. But looking back now, separated by the decades, I have a deeper appreciation for the once-in-a-lifetime nature of the event—how it helped shape the US Chamber's image as an emerging new force, domestically and abroad, and how it was a formative step in my emerging tenure.

But there was still much that I wanted to set in motion outside the glare of the world press corps and international politics. One such initiative was the National Chamber Litigation Center, another offshoot of the Powell Memorandum that we launched in 1977. The Center was the only public policy law firm that strictly represented American business interests in cases involving regulatory agencies and the courts. Powell had noted that consumer advocate Nader and other activists had public interest law firms in their corners and, if Nader and Co. didn't win on Capitol Hill, they took their crusades to court. That sounded like a strategy we should employ as well, as a way of counteracting antibusiness legal cases.

We set up a program that, in short order, began scoring important victories on issues involving striker replacement, prevailing wages, punitive damages, Superfund liability, and government contracts. Of some four hundred cases the NCLC would take on in its first twenty years, 60 percent achieved precedent-setting decisions for business. Today, the NCLC remains the most successful litigation program ever created by any entity. When organizations petition the Supreme Court, the Court accepts about 2 percent of those cases—and, during my watch, cases brought by the US Chamber were accepted roughly 80 percent of the time. But even more impressive, we won on average 75 percent of them.

I had the privilege of hearing about our track record for success from a man who was well acquainted with it—US Supreme Court Chief Justice Warren Burger. We had lunch several times in his private dining room in the Supreme Court building and I found that he enjoyed talking about the issues of the day as much as I did. At the time, it didn't dawn on me that there were probably ten thousand lawyers in Washington who would have liked to have that opportunity—I simply was honored to be invited for a bite to eat and a chance to chew the fat with one of the most powerful individuals in the United States.

The chief justice told me during these lunch sessions that the court took a high percentage of our cases for several reasons: the justices always looked forward to a case brought by the Chamber because, first of all, they knew it would be important and, secondly, they could count on it being extremely well formulated. There was a reason for both. We got the best lawyers in the country to represent us and they worked for us pro bono. Before they ever set foot in the Supreme Court to make their arguments, we staged "moot court" sessions at the Chamber to prepare them for any conceivable twist that might arise. We never wasted the court's time with frivolous arguments. It was no accident that members of the court looked forward to the Chamber participating in a case—and why we made such an impact in the legal arena. It was fairly inexpensive to pursue this approach, but extremely important in establishing a strong voice for business.

One such case that still sticks with me involved the state of Oklahoma, which had passed a law preventing foreigners from buying land in the state. The Oklahoma Chamber of Commerce opposed that barrier and so did we, aware that it would have destroyed the free flow of trade and investment. The short version of the story is that the case involved a Canadian company and we prevailed in front of the Supreme Court, protecting the firm's right to purchase land in Oklahoma. The principle we were fighting for might appear somewhat strange, but it was extremely important. On the one hand, many farmers and ranchers in Oklahoma were afraid that land values would be priced out of reach if foreign companies were allowed in as buyers. Their fear notwithstanding, it was a bad law for business and trade, prompting our involvement in what we regarded as a landmark case. The fact was, we would not take up a company's issue and pursue it before the highest court in the land unless the case had broad implications for the future strength of US business.

Though many of the cases we took on didn't receive big national attention, almost all of them got some kind of national press. Gradually, word spread that the Chamber was *doing* something—and the results we achieved were tangible to business people. They saw the outcomes, understanding and appreciating our efforts. From a personal perspective, I certainly had a great deal of appreciation for the individual who had helped pave the way, former Justice Lewis Powell. I spoke with him on the phone once and invited him down to speak at the Chamber. Powell declined, but he knew what we were doing and clearly approved of it.

One of my guideposts from the start was my unwavering conviction against raising taxes. In fact, in my very first Chamber meeting when I took the job in 1975, I told my staff that I'd counted at least one hundred different issues on our plate. "We're probably going to make a mistake once in a while," I stated. "But I want to tell you, don't ever make a mistake on taxation. That's been the number one issue all the way back to the Boston Tea Party." And, as you will read later in these pages, I was prepared to fight for that tenet, regardless of the consequences.

My schedule at the Chamber, meanwhile, couldn't have been busier, as you might imagine from our work on so many fronts. It helped that I had a top-notch team around me, including the administrative assistant I had brought over to the Chamber from the National Center for Resource Recovery, Agnes Plocki, who did a marvelous job keeping my appointments organized and my hectic schedule on track. I worked at the office from 7:00 a.m. to 7:00 p.m., which is what I'd always done at NASA and NCRR. My dedication stemmed from the work ethic that began when I worked my way through high school and later college, graduate school, and my doctoral program. It was always an integral part of the process for me, and it certainly served me well now.

In addition to all the lobbying and legal cases we undertook, the Chamber published *Nation's Business* magazine, the oldest and largest-circulation monthly magazine in the country. We put out a newspaper and a weekly radio program, which I always appeared on, and our building was buzzing with breakfast and luncheon meetings almost every day of the week. Our kitchen, along with caterers we utilized, served thousands of meals each year. Whenever a foreign delegation arrived to visit the White House, the group of dignitaries usually ended up on the Chamber's schedule as well. The reason why countries send representatives to see our president is, first and foremost, because of economic considerations. They want trade and investment. As a result, we wound up hosting foreign delegations on a weekly basis. I had twelve hundred people working for me—and all of us worked tirelessly in the energizing, exciting atmosphere of the reshaped Chamber.

I'll always remember the time President Zia-ul-Haq of Pakistan visited the Chamber. I struck up a friendship with him and he invited me to visit his country. I finally made the trip after some five years had passed. When he greeted me at his palace doorway, the television cameras were running and I remarked, "President Zia, you look younger than you did five years ago. What's your secret?" He smiled and answered, "I have a secret, Dr. Lesher, and I'll share it with everybody once we're all seated." Once we had taken our seats inside, the president stood up and pronounced, "Dr. Lesher told me how young I look and he wants to know my secret. I will share my secret with all of you. I have discovered golf! I have discovered that if you put your troubles in your desk door, and play golf two times a week . . ."

I interjected, smiling broadly: "Excuse me, sir. My intelligence says you play more than two times a week." He laughed and played right along, saying, "You have very good intelligence, Dr. Lesher." Everyone in the room roared at our playful back-and-forth, and the festive mood continued as the president told a golf joke. Naturally, I followed with one of my own. We each told several more, much to the enjoyment of the crowd. After such a wonderful meeting, you can imagine how shocked and saddened I was several months later after the news that he and the American ambassador who'd hosted me for a lunch had been killed when the helicopter in which they were flying was sabotaged.

Another memorable visit involved the prime minister of India, Rajiv Gandhi. My staff had worked with his staff for a month to prepare for his much-anticipated visit. When the day finally arrived, the Chamber building was abuzz with excitement and a packed press contingent. The schedule began with a closed session with the prime minister, Chamber leadership, and CEOs of companies doing business in India or wanting to develop operations there. It was completely off the record, and Gandhi gave an informal speech and fielded a multitude of questions. When the meeting finally ended, his aides were nowhere in sight and he turned to me to ask what the next item was on the agenda. "It's the press conference," I said matter-of-factly. "*What* press conference?" he replied with a look of complete surprise.

After all of the planning for his arrival, nobody on his staff had told Gandhi that he would also be facing the national media. A roomful of reporters awaited to pepper him with questions just a few feet down the hallway. "Nobody told me about this—what should I do?" he asked me. Without hesitation, I said, "I'd suggest you make a few informal remarks and hit on only the things you want to talk about. If you just go in and take questions, they can come at you from anywhere." The prime minister seemed to relax upon hearing my strategy. "Oh that's good, I can do that," he said. And he proceeded to enter the room and his session with the press was a rousing success. I was glad I could lend this very nice world leader a hand—stemming from all my experience dealing with pressure-packed Washington situations—in a tough spot.

All in all, I traveled to eighty-five countries with the Chamber, and experienced many moments that were memorable for all manner of reasons. One such trip was to Taiwan, where I sang at a lavish dinner in a gathering hosted by the head of the Taiwan Chamber, a Mr. Wong. He was quite an extravagant, wealthy fellow and his wife had a marvelous voice. She sang before dinner and then I was informed it was tradition that someone from the American delegation had to sing after dinner.

I wasn't going to risk offending anyone, so I volunteered and regaled the group with a version of *San Antonio Rose*. The husband was so excited by all of this that he stood up and sang too, prompting his sons to remark that they'd never seen him have so much fun. The next year I visited, my host was ready. He'd taken singing lessons and couldn't wait to perform. He even hired a twelve-piece orchestra to play before dinner, and asked me to respond afterwards. I was glad to oblige, once again belting out the Bob Wills tune to the crowd's delight.

On a more serious note, I traveled with a small delegation to Zimbabwe soon after it declared independence from Great Britain and changed its name from Rhodesia. I met with President Robert Mugabe, a Cambridge-educated, highly sophisticated man. On behalf of our group, I asked him what kind of economy he intended to run. He said, "Well, I'm going to run a pragmatic, socialist economy." I didn't try to mask my skepticism, responding "What, pray tell is that?" I'll never forget his answer: "It's very much like what you have in America—a role for business and a role for government." Of course, Mugabe didn't define what percentage each would have, and wound up taking what had been the most prosperous nation in all of Africa and ruining it after thirty years with his misguided socialist approach. If there's ever a stark example of how socialism doesn't hold a candle to capitalism, Mugabe's utter destruction of the former bread basket of Africa is it.

On a trip to Panama, we arrived late for a meeting with the president and were greeted by motorcycle policemen and a stretch limousine waiting for our whole group. It was 4:00 p.m. and the highway was absolutely jammed in both lanes, so the lead motorcycle policeman drove down the center of them—forcing buses and trucks to the shoulder, as if he was separating the waters for us to pass down the middle. When we arrived within the city limits, the policeman stopped traffic in all directions at every intersection, until we managed to leapfrog our way to the palace. This royal traffic treatment by the police was actually far more exciting than our meeting with the president.

I traveled often to the Dominican Republic. On one such visit, I had come for a meeting of AACCLA—the Association of American Chambers of Commerce in Latin America, a very powerful organization despite the fact that most people have never heard of it. It consists of American executives who live in a given Latin American country and most are associated with large, powerful companies. Consequently, those companies represent a large piece of the gross national product in those countries. On this particular visit, I met with the Dominican Republic president—an elderly man who had lost his vision—to tell him about the Chamber's satellite operations. I wanted to convey the high-tech educational benefits of satellite broadcasts to combat illiteracy, a major problem in his country. I explained to him how the Chamber was utilizing satellite-transmitted shows to teach groups in the United States and he was fascinated. "If you implemented this here, you wouldn't have to hire nearly as many teachers or build as many schools," I said to him. He seemed so excited by this idea and its potential for educating his citizenry—the majority of whom, he noted, already watched commercial television as a way of learning. I don't know what came of our discussion, but I felt moved by his plight as leader of such a poor nation and very much wanted to help this kind man.

I traveled to Japan some twenty times because they were one of our primary trading partners, and the Japanese also spent a great deal of money advertising with the Chamber. We often conducted two-way international teleconferences from Chamber studios to studios in Tokyo, featuring the CEOs from Sony and other Japanese companies discussing trade and investment. We would always meet with the US ambassador to whatever country we visited, and in Japan that was, during the Carter and Reagan years, former Democratic senator from Montana, Mike Mansfield. He was such a nice, humble man—he wouldn't ever call his secretary to serve coffee or tea; he'd get up and serve it himself. He was a perfect host.

On one of my visits with the Japanese prime minister, my interpreter was a lovely woman working in Japan's equivalent of the state department. A photograph of the three of us appeared on the front page of virtually every newspaper in Japan a few years later when her engagement to the Crown Prince was announced. Since then, I've always enjoyed telling my friends a real-life princess served as my personal interpreter.

When I wasn't traveling during this formative period, I made a point of changing more than our approach to policy matters and the initiatives we tackled. When it came to personnel, I moved very deliberately in assessing my staff—purposely not coming in and firing people, but rather slowly weeding out those I felt held us back, while bringing in the best people I could find to help us move forward. But I also sent a message with one of my first personnel decisions. The director of personnel came to see about the receptionist in our lobby.

"What's the problem?" I said.

"Well, the previous receptionist left and we've been interviewing for a replacement, and the person who's come to the top of the list is Jeanette Smith," he explained.

"Why are you bringing this to me?" I replied, dumbfounded.

"Well," he replied in a semi-whisper, "she's *black*."

"Is she the best-qualified person?" I asked sternly.

The director affirmed that she was indeed, and I looked him squarely in the eyes and said, "What the hell are you waiting for? *Hire* her."

That was a signature hire, because it let everybody in the building know that we weren't going to tolerate bias of any kind—whether racial or gender—in personnel management. When I looked back on my years with the Chamber, I regard that as a defining moment, the sign that we welcomed people of all races and countries. You need to realize that when I arrived, the Chamber was entrenched in the past. The men all wore white shirts and ties, suits and hats, and an air of the Old South still permeated the organization. The only black employees when I took over were relegated to basement jobs—support staff for the printing press and the mailroom.

But by the time I left twenty-two years later, our staff included many African-Americans, as well as employees from the Far East, Middle East, and South America—and a large percentage of women. When I joined the Chamber, we had only one or two. When I departed, I'm proud to say that half of my professional staff was female. I made more than a few speeches to my staff, particularly my vice presidents, making clear that our policy was simple: find the best person, whoever they were, and go with it.

As the decade wound to a close, and I neared my fifth year on the job, big changes were afoot—both for the Chamber and for me. In 1979, we launched a new initiative, rapidly propelling us to a new level of visibility and clout: a national television show dealing with pressing business and economic issues, taped each week from a studio inside the Chamber building. The program, *It's Your Business*, was syndicated each Sunday across the country.

With Anheuser-Busch serving as our sponsor, *It's Your Business* quickly became a highly popular program among politicians, business leaders, and anybody interested in issues with an impact on the nation's economy. We created the show in the format of a weekly debate, with guests on both sides of the aisle from the House, Senate, and cabinet, as well as leading figures in labor unions and the national media. Our advisors argued strongly that the same Chamber representative should appear each week, so I was "elected." As you know, I always enjoyed a good fight—and had no trepidation joining the debate each week to tussle with guests on behalf of the business perspective.

At the same time, a seasoned politician who understood the power of television—having made a career on the screen in movies and TV—was rising to the forefront of American politics. Ronald Reagan earned the Republican nomination for president in the summer of 1980. Reagan was on the verge of orchestrating major changes—for the United States and the entire world.

Furthermore, he was about to fundamentally change my own life as well—both personally and professionally. I would soon have a wonderful new ally in the White House with President Reagan, and a powerful and exciting new way of transmitting the message we shared with him.

7 A New Show in Town

SOMETIME AFTER 2:00 a.m., as the greater Washington, DC, area slept, a voice familiar to radio listeners across the United States beamed over the airwaves from a red-carpeted, twelfth-floor studio in Arlington, Virginia. Popular talk show host Larry King was in the midst of one of his countless interviews on the only national radio call-in program going in 1979, an overnight show on the Mutual Broadcasting System reaching six million loyal followers. King's conversational interviews with all manner of newsmakers—and rough-hewn baritone from years of heavy smoking—were signature elements of his hit program.

On this particular night, his guest on "The Larry King Show" was a man who had been making quite a bit of news as president of the United States Chamber of Commerce. Dick Lesher didn't have the recognizable timbre of the veteran host, but he'd given a distinct voice to the US Chamber in barely four years on the job. And King wanted to talk to the Chamber's driving force about issues facing the economy—and how those factors might influence the course of the 1980 presidential election.

Lesher took the opportunity to predict the coming of a new age of conservatism that would push incumbent Jimmy Carter out of office and see a revitalization of business in the country.

"The public is fed up with big government and over-regulation and too much taxation," he proclaimed. Calls began lighting up the AT&T switchboard from around the country, with one listener after the next eager to speak with Lesher and express excitement over the prospect of change. But within a matter of minutes, the switchboard inexplicably shut down. It turns out that an avalanche of people calling at the same time in the wee hours—energized by the message from the nation's number one businessman—had overloaded the circuits.

The segment continued without callers, but plenty of listeners. The interview was such a smashing success, in fact, that King invited Lesher back a year later to re-address the topic. Once again, the dialogue began after 2:00 a.m., but this time, the lights on the switchboard barely flickered—and technical problems had nothing to do with the surprising lack of calls.

Following his appearance, Lesher realized what had happened. His views against big government had no doubt struck a chord with many listeners the first time around, but now the same theme was being espoused on a daily basis by someone else with a considerably larger pulpit: the Republican presidential standard *bearer, Ronald Reagan. Americans hungry for the conservative perspective were getting more than their fill from the GOP candidate's well-honed oratory on the stump—and clearly no longer felt moved to make calls in the dead of night to express their solidarity with the leader of the US Chamber.*

Lesher chuckled at the revelation. He had absolutely no problem with his thunder being stolen by Reagan, a candidate he believed would lead the way for a new era of business prosperity in America—and put the country back on track.

On the night before the election in 1980, I happened to be out of the country on business, meeting with officials from the American Chambers in Latin American. I had just given some prepared remarks at a luncheon and the first question zeroed right in on the race for the White House. "Who's going to win the election tomorrow?" someone asked me.

"Well, don't believe what you read in the paper, because they're all wrong," I replied bluntly. "Ronald Reagan will be the next president. He'll win in a landslide and sweep ten well-known names out of the Senate. I named them—and I wound up being wrong on only two of them!"

The fact was, many news outlets were predicting a very close win for Carter, but I didn't buy that—basing my views on the constant discussions I was having regularly with Republican political leaders. As the election neared, we became increasingly convinced that the tide had shifted to Reagan's favor. I saw further evidence during my trip to Latin America, when I happened to run into my old friend Esther Peterson, the member of Carter's staff with whom I had clashed on occasion. She had been out campaigning heavily for Carter, but looked worried. "What's the matter, Esther?" I asked. And her answer confirmed everything I'd been thinking. "We have no chance," she said quietly.

In the end, Carter's greatest accomplishment—orchestrating the peace accord between Egypt and Israel—was overshadowed by the stagnant economy and his own inability to articulate a sense of hope to Americans worried about the worst inflation we'd *ever* seen, rising interest rates, the high cost of gasoline, and the general direction of the country.

Fighting that battle is right at the heart of everything the Chamber stood for—with our goal to reduce spending and over-regulation to get the economy moving forward again. Amid all of that, the most damaging thing Carter did was to talk about the malaise of America—as if our best years were behind us. It's essential for the president of the United States to always metaphorically plant the flag on the hill and express a positive attitude even when times are tough. President Kennedy, for all the challenges he faced during his three years in office, understood that perfectly. He knew it was his job to buck up America and stress the bright future that lay ahead. This was Ronald Reagan's gift as well, and it connected so deeply with the electorate that his landslide victory over Carter had become an inevitability.

Contrary to what you might think, the US Chamber never took a public stance in support of Reagan during the election, or took any position during the race. Despite my personal beliefs, I insisted that we act as a non-partisan organization. In the House or Senate, we would occasionally support a Democratic candidate if they met our pro-business criteria. We were involved in many House and Senate races and won an overwhelming number of them—all building blocks in what would become a foundation of the Reagan Revolution.

Even before Reagan was elected, his people reached out to us at the US Chamber—due to the close ties they had with the state of California's Chamber of Commerce. It was a smart move on their part, because we were able to brief them on pressing business issues prior to Reagan winning the election. This also established a comfortable and friendly relationship between our two camps. And very soon after Reagan beat Carter, even *prior* to the inauguration, he flew into Washington and held a dinner party at the F Street Club for what he called his "new neighbors." He invited Maryland governor Harry Hughes, Virginia governor John Dalton, Washington, DC, mayor Marion Barry, a handful of other local politicians—and myself. "I just wanted to meet all of you folks," he told us. It was a pleasant, casual dinner and, when we were finished eating, we all gathered around the president and he began swapping jokes with us. That was the beginning of my relationship with him and I still remember his first joke.

A woman was on the delivery table and looked up at her doctor and said, "Doctor, will this pain last very long?" And the doctor looked at her solemnly and replied, "I'm afraid so—about eighteen years." That, I quickly learned, was his kind of material—quick, punchy, and nothing that couldn't be repeated in open company. It happened to be my kind of joke as well, and we would share many others during the years to come.

On a personal note, my life had taken a truly wonderful turn by then. I had gradually fallen in love with the woman who kept my work life in order—Agnes, and we married in June 1981. My first marriage, as I indicated earlier, had continued to deteriorate under the intense pressures and commitments of my career and ended in divorce. As my administrative assistant, Agnes fully understood the heavy load I faced on an almost hourly basis—working at the top level of business and politics—and was an invaluable support to me. Agnes was not only an excellent assistant with a natural gift for organization and communication, but beautiful and charming. And as my wife, she remained on the job until the day I retired, always offering wise and trusted counsel—and always a hit at the many high-level functions we attended together.

Right after the inauguration, Agnes and I were invited by the president for a White House dinner, along with three dozen other guests. I wound up sitting next to Nancy Reagan and, in an effort to strike up a casual conversation, accidentally put my foot in my mouth. Quick background for this story: soon after moving into the White House, the First Lady had been criticized in the press for ordering fancy new china. Now, sitting beside her at dinner, I thought I could break the ice with a light-hearted reference to the situation, remarking, "Is this the new china?" Her back straightened and her expression stiffened. I knew instantly that I had taken an ill-advised tack in our small talk, so I moved immediately to change course.

"Excuse me, let me start over again," I said. "I was trying to make a dumb joke, but let me tell you what the American public thinks about that china—and everything else you're doing with this beautiful institution. After the Carter years, everyone is applauding everything you do—so just go right on and keep doing it." Senator Paul Laxalt's wife, who was seated to my other side, buoyed my attempt at a recovery. "That's it, Dick—that's what I've been telling her!" With that, the rest of the dinner talk proceeded swimmingly and Nancy relaxed—though I learned right then that while the president possessed a great sense of humor, she did not. Mrs. Reagan was far more serious, and fully dedicated to making her husband look good at all times. I should add one footnote to the evening. After a lovely dinner, we all moved to the White House movie theater—a decidedly tough ticket to get in Washington. The entire group went downstairs and took our seats and enjoyed a first showing of *The French Lieutenant's Woman*, starring Meryl Streep and Jeremy Irons.

Soon after that dinner, we reciprocated with a dinner at the Chamber for the entire Reagan cabinet—including such names as Secretary of State Alexander Haig, Secretary of Defense Caspar Weinberger, Secretary of Commerce Malcolm Baldridge, Secretary of Transportation Drew Lewis, Secretary of Education Terrell Bell, Secretary of Health and Human Services Richard Schweiker, Attorney General William French Smith, Secretary of the Interior James Watt, Director of the Office of Management and Budget David Stockman, Assistant to the President Elizabeth Dole, and more. It was an A-list dinner that anyone in government would have been thrilled to attend. The funny thing is this: I can barely remember anything about it, likely because I was so immersed in so many introductory conversations. But I do know the evening helped create more personal relationships with Reagan's team, an important step as I guided the Chamber in these new, promising waters with a friendly, pro-business administration.

From that point on, Reagan's new counselor to the president, Edwin Meese, Chief of Staff Jim Baker, and other top brass from the White House were regular visitors to my dining room at the Chamber for personal briefings and to establish relationships. What a contrast to my experience with Carter and his crew! We tied in seamlessly with their objectives because our program for rebuilding America mirrored their own, chapter and verse. Both Reagan and I had been giving the same talk about big government and over-regulation and the imperative to change all those old patterns. Now we were working in concert to do just that.

Right off the bat, I developed a warm and easy rapport with the president—with joke-telling a regular part of our dealings. Among the many papers I subscribed to and read each day was my hometown paper from Chambersburg, the *Public Opinion*. One day, the paper ran excerpts of various essays that Catholic school first-graders in Chambersburg had written about President Reagan. They were quite amusing, so I sent them over to Reagan with a little note attached that read, "This will lighten your day, Mr. President." By God, he called me right up when he received it—just to talk about those letters from the kids and how they had brightened his day, indeed. One child had mistakenly assumed that the president dealt with animals at the zoo, and I interjected, "I like that one the most. Little does he know how right he is about you dealing with animals." We shared a good laugh about that—and I thought to myself how amazing it was to have just received a call from the president of the United States to chuckle over some children's writings.

Of course, the laughter and hopeful spirit was nearly cut short on March 30, 1981, when would-be assassin John Hinckley Jr. fired on the president outside the Washington Hilton hotel. I was at the Chamber when we received word of this shocking moment in history. Press Secretary James Brady had the most serious casualty, left paralyzed by the attack. But the president was also wounded—struck by a bullet that entered his chest, causing initially undetected internal bleeding. The injury might well have been fatal if not for the split-second decision to detour to George Washington University Medical Center, where he received prompt, life-saving attention.

All of those who had gotten to know the president during such a brief time in office, only sixty-nine days, felt numb. But he was strong and determined and made a remarkably speedy recovery—a blessing for the country—and our fruitful dealings with the administration continued to flourish. My own relationship with the president and his staff grew as well, both at work and at play. That opened the door to invitations to memorable state dinners at the White House and to a particularly enjoyable experience on multiple occasions—playing tennis on the White House courts. Reagan didn't play, but other members of his administration did, and that led to tennis invitations from Reagan's speechwriter Ben Elliott, the First Lady's Chief of Staff Jim Rosebush, future secretary of commerce (and former chairman of the US Chamber of Commerce) Bill Verity, and my good friend Jack Kemp, the congressman from New York turned secretary of housing and urban development.

I was always an avid and competitive tennis player, so you can imagine what a thrill it was to find myself whacking balls on the most exclusive court in the country. As an aside, my favorite tennis partner during my Chamber years was Kemp, who directed HUD in the administration of George H. W. Bush from 1989 to 1993. Jack and his wife, Joanne, lived within walking distance of us in

Bethesda, Maryland, in a wooded neighborhood on Bradley Boulevard where I had my own personal tennis court. One day he called and said he needed some advice on an issue. "Give me five minutes to shower and come on over," I told him. I jumped in the shower and the next thing I remember was Agnes yelling to me, "Hurry Dick, Jack is caught underneath his car in the driveway!"

I threw on my clothes and ran outside of our house, which was located on a hill. It turns out he had just pulled into our driveway and stepped out of his car, thinking he'd put it in park, but he had neglected to do that and it started rolling backwards down the drive. Instead of reaching in to hit the brake, he apparently thought he still possessed the agility that made him a great NFL quarterback with the Buffalo Bills—and thrust his foot inside the moving car to push the brake pedal. But he lost his balance, got his foot caught, and wound up getting pulled down the hill. The car veered off the driveway and hit a tree, otherwise he might have been hurt very badly. Fortunately, he only wound up skinning his elbows and knees. Joanne hurried over and still had to take him to the ER at Suburban Hospital to get him properly bandaged up. After that, Jack went around town telling people, "Lesher tried to kill me!"

The truth is, Jack and I were close friends. As evidence of that, a friend one day asked me, "Dick, can you name ten people in Congress you would trust with your life in a foxhole?"

My first response was, "Wow, that's a tough question!" But then I went on to name eight or ten people, including Senators Richard Lugar of Indiana and Connie Mack of Florida. Later that same week, Agnes and I were having dinner with Jack and Joanne. I asked Jack the same question I'd been asked and his response was exactly the same as mine—"Wow, that's a tough question!" The punch line was that we each named five of the same people. The one person we each had in common, perhaps not surprisingly given his toughness and war hero status: Bob Dole.

My relationship with Kemp was considerably warmer than my initial dealings with Elizabeth Dole, in her capacity as special assistant to the president for public liaison. In the early phase of Reagan's administration, she began calling the heads of various organizations, inviting them for personal meetings with her at the White House. I received an invitation and gladly went over for my get-to-know-you session, eager to lay the groundwork for a solid working relationship. After several minutes of friendly banter, she said, "Dick, if you want to meet with anyone in this administration, you call me and I'll set it up for you."

Those were not words I wanted to hear, especially given the fact that I'd already developed good relationships with various members of Reagan's staff—and didn't need her help to get in touch with anyone I might want to talk to about a given topic. "No, Elizabeth, I don't think that'll work," I responded. "I and all my staff have already built a relationship with all the cabinet and sub-cabinet. We've had them over for briefings. We know them." I made it clear to her that I didn't want to waste time getting her to make my contacts for me.

Up until that moment she had been quite cordial, but immediately her demeanor changed. She stood up, looked me square in the eyes and said sternly, "Now you listen here. You will go through me if you want access to members of the administration." With that, I stood up and answered back in a similar no-nonsense tone: "Now *you* listen here. I'm trying to do you a favor to keep you from making a big mistake. And your tactic is a *huge* mistake. If your colleagues hear you're trying to do this, they'll come down all over you—all you'll be doing is impeding communications." After that, I never bothered to go through her as she'd demanded—nor did I have any trouble getting access to whomever I needed. Other business leaders, on the other hand, acceded to her ground rules and, not surprisingly, had constant trouble getting appointments with anyone.

I'll say this about Elizabeth Dole: she was, and is, a tough lady and a brilliant person. But this was a difficult role for her, as she tried to establish a foothold for power on a team essentially being run by Baker and Meese. The reality was that she was simply not integral to their plans and they later moved her to a more important and higher-profile role: secretary of transportation. In that job, she did marvelous work, pushing through expansion projects at Dulles and National Airports that had been languishing for years. Later, she became secretary of labor under Bush, the first woman to serve in two different cabinet positions under two presidents.

Despite our heated introductory meeting, Elizabeth and I became good friends. She and her husband, Senator Bob Dole—a man and a friend I deeply admire to this day—invited Agnes and me to their Sunday brunch at the Watergate, and there were never any lingering hard feelings. We often arranged special events in our Hall of Flags auditorium for Elizabeth to address visiting groups in the Chamber building—just across Lafayette Square park from the White House. We brought a lot of politicians into that auditorium, which featured flags of the great commercial explorers. Long before he became a fixture as speaker of the House, when he was still basically unknown, we brought Newt Gingrich to speak there many times. Newt also wound up being a guest on at least a dozen occasions on the television show, *It's Your Business*—an endeavor that quickly became a signature element of the new Chamber, raising our profile to new heights across the nation.

Best wishes to Dick Lesher --
Jimmy Carter

Plate 01. President Jimmy Carter and I didn't always see eye to eye and he made it clear from the start that he was no fan of the US Chamber of Commerce, but we did our best to work together on policies impacting American business as you can see from this White House meeting where we converse from across the conference table.

Plate 02. There was no president of the United States I respected more than Ronald Reagan. His ability to connect with people, and our shared love of a good joke, created a special bond between the two of us.

Plate 03. A big part of my job was holding Congress accountable to business in its votes and legislation and that often made me a thorn in the side of Senate Majority Leader Tip O'Neill.

For Dick Lesher - With admiration! Walter Cronkite, February 1979

Plate 04. I made a point of having lunch every year or so with legendary CBS anchor Walter Cronkite during my Chamber years. He was always fond of talking about NASA.

late 05. The dance skills I acquired in high school served me well throughout my life, especially at the many social functions that later became part of my life. Fortunately, I found a wonderful dance partner in my wife, Agnes, who could cut a rug as well as I could!

Plate 06. Hunting was always a passion in my life, with roots to my early childhood. I've had many a loyal hunting dog over the years. Sadly, we recently lost our sweet, sixteen-year-old Brittany Spaniel, Duchess. But my faithful dog Remy, a German Shorthaired Pointer, adds much joy to our lives and I rely on him mightily on hunting trips.

THE WHITE HOUSE

WASHINGTON

February 18, 1982

Dear Dick:

Thank you very much for your warm response
to my State of the Union message. The help
of many Americans in demonstrating public
support for our Program for Economic Recovery
last year was a major part of our first steps
on the road to national renewal. Sustaining
the public trust that we built during the
past year will require a stable economic
policy on those of us serving in positions
of public trust.

The next few months will not be easy ones as
we continue our work on the major initiatives
that we have started. I deeply appreciate
the approval that you have expressed so
frequently, and I'll continue working to
justify your enduring support.

With all my best wishes,

Sincerely,

Ron

Dr. Richard L. Lesher
President
Chamber of Commerce of the
   United States of America
1615 H Street, N.W.
Washington, D.C. 20062

Plate 07. A letter from President Reagan thanking me for a note I'd written him about his State of the Union Address.

THE WHITE HOUSE

WASHINGTON

September 3, 1981

Dear Dick:

From the bottom of my heart I want to express my gratitude to you for all that you did to assist the passage of our bipartisan Program for Economic Recovery. Elizabeth Dole has told me of your hard work which contributed to this victory for the American people. Only a superb team effort could have produced the demonstration of public support necessary for this success, and I am grateful that you were part of our team.

Thanks to you, we have begun our historic journey toward national renewal. I am confident that the revival of the American economy will enhance the spirit of our people and restore the vision of a prosperous republic so cherished by our Founding Fathers. We have achieved a great deal together already. I would like to continue our partnership for the American people.

Sincerely,

Ron

Dr. Richard Lesher
President
U.S. Chamber of Commerce
1615 H Street, N.W.
Washington, D.C. 20062

Plate o8. Another prized letter from President Reagan, expressing thanks for assisting with passage of the Program for Economic Recovery.

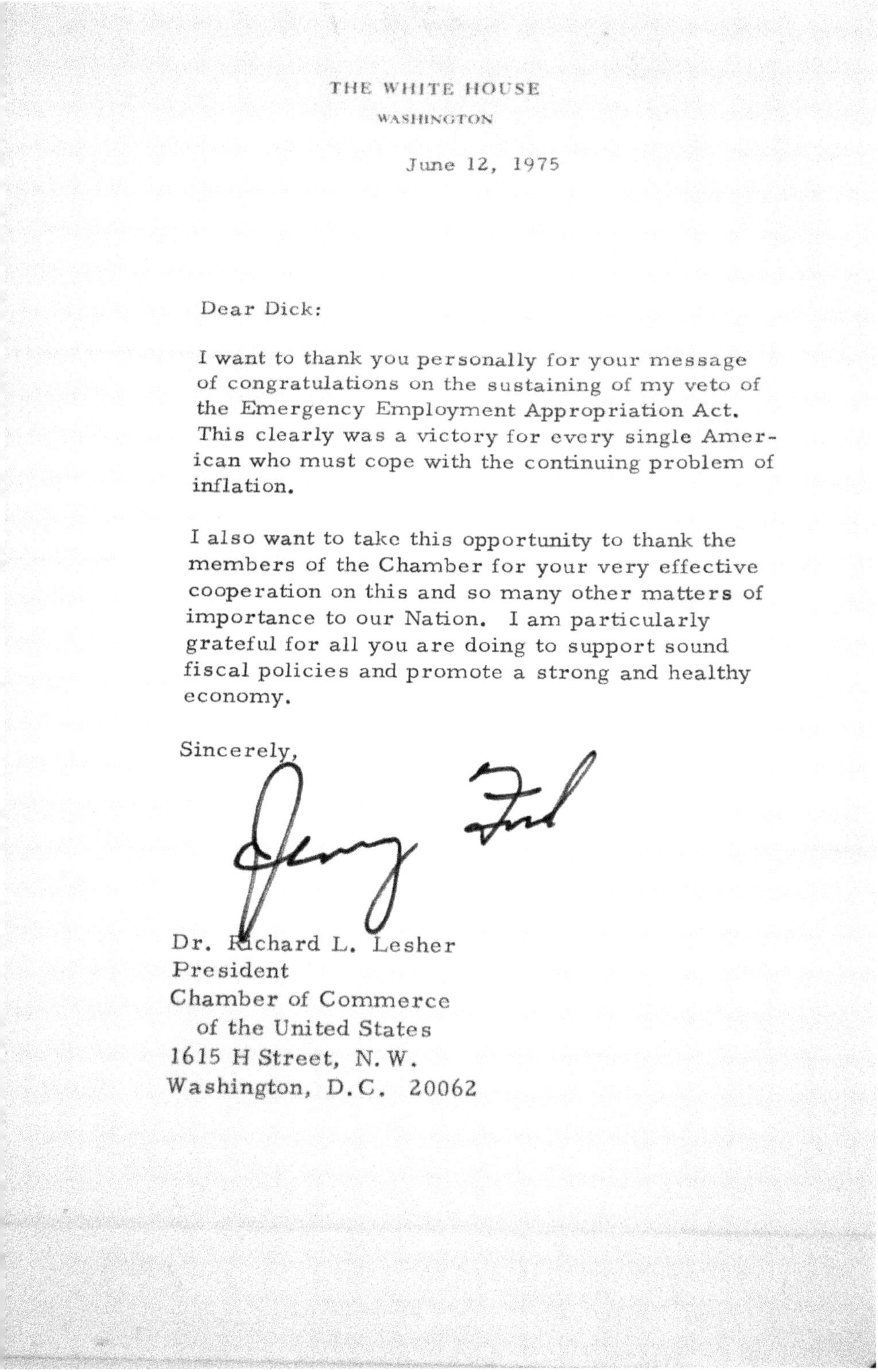

THE WHITE HOUSE

WASHINGTON

June 12, 1975

Dear Dick:

I want to thank you personally for your message
of congratulations on the sustaining of my veto of
the Emergency Employment Appropriation Act.
This clearly was a victory for every single American who must cope with the continuing problem of
inflation.

I also want to take this opportunity to thank the
members of the Chamber for your very effective
cooperation on this and so many other matters of
importance to our Nation. I am particularly
grateful for all you are doing to support sound
fiscal policies and promote a strong and healthy
economy.

Sincerely,

Jerry Ford

Dr. Richard L. Lesher
President
Chamber of Commerce
  of the United States
1615 H Street, N.W.
Washington, D.C. 20062

Plate 09. One of my first presidential letters, this one from Gerald Ford thanking me for writing him about his
veto of the Emergency Employment Appropriation Act.

Plate 10. My trip to Egypt to visit with the country's new president, Hosni Mubarak, came only three weeks after the assassination of Anwar Sadat. Mubarak, who had been vice president, was insistent on not cancelling our meeting because he wanted to give the impression to the world that life in Egypt was back to normal. The former Egyptian Air Force pilot was eager to talk business and further American business interests with his country.

Plate 11. I worked well with President George H. W. Bush and he was a frequent visitor to Chamber headquarters to utilize our television studios. We appeared together on multiple occasions to answer questions from the White House press corps.

THE WHITE HOUSE

WASHINGTON

October 29, 1981

Dear Dick:

Mentioning your continued support during my
October 1 news conference was only a small
token of the gratitude that I feel for the
activities of the Chamber of Commerce this
year. You have been with us through every
step of the path that we have charted toward
economic recovery, and I deeply appreciate
your willingness to continue that support.
I know that we have a way to go, but we are
moving in the right direction. Thanks very
much for everything that you have contributed
to our efforts.

With my best wishes and warmest regards,

Sincerely,

Ron

Mr. Richard L. Lesher
President
Chamber of Commerce of the
   United States of America
1615 H Street, N.W.
Washington, D.C. 20062

Plate 12. Another kind note of thanks from President Reagan, expressing gratitude for the support we gave him early in his first term.

Plate 13. One of the highlights of my tenure at the Chamber was hosting lavish functions connected to the Egypt-Israel Peace Treaty brokered by President Carter in 1977—a dinner in Washington for Egyptian President Anwar Sadat and luncheon in New York City for Menachem Begin, pictured here. It was exhilarating to find myself in the middle of this historic moment.

To Dick Lesher
with best wishes,
Geo Bush

Plate 14. I enjoyed working with our forty-first President, George H. W. Bush, though, as vice president, he once called me from Air Force Two to lobby me to support President Reagan's proposed tax increase— something I was highly opposed to.

Plate 15. President Bill Clinton and I were often on different sides of the political fence, but I always found him to be personable and someone who had an understanding of the Chamber's influence. He, like Reagan and Bush before him, utilized our high-tech television studios—and that did not sit well at all with the Republican Congress, which, in turn, gave me ample political headaches.

Plate 16. Bob Dole was a man who knew how to get things done and working with him was a pleasure. I'll never forget the compliment he paid me after my retirement when he told a crowd that I ran the Chamber "with great integrity."

late 17. Gerald Ford was the first US president I worked with and he penned a very gracious foreword for my book, *Economic Progress . . . It's Everybody's Business.*

Plate 18. Don't let the smile on President Jimmy Carter's face fool you. He and First Lady Rosalynn were not at all excited to meet the new president of the US Chamber.

Plate 19. I'm very fond of this photo filming a promo for *It's Your Business*—because it contains two of my favorite people from that era: moderator Meryl Comer and HUD secretary and former US representative Jack Kemp, both quality and talented individuals.

Plate 20. One of the benefits of my job was getting to know and interact with many top-notch legislators, such as Arizona senator and Vietnam war hero John McCain.

To Richard Lesher
With best wishes,

Nancy Reagan

Plate 21. First Lady Nancy Reagan and I got along swimmingly, though I started our relationship by accidentally offending with her a quip about the fancy White House china she had ordered. Fortunately, I redeemed myself and we enjoyed a great relationship after that.

Plate 22. President Reagan was genuinely interested in creating a strong relationship with the US Chamber and we were often in his presence. Here I am with then chairman of the Chamber, Ed Donley (second from left)—a wonderful man who was a pleasure to work with.

Plate 23. Being in the presence of Ronald Reagan, a great president and a man I considered a friend, never
got old.

Plate 24. Hosting a gala dinner for Egyptian President Anwar Sadat at the US Chamber of Commerce building, who was visiting Washington to sign the momentous Egypt-Israel Peace Treaty with Israeli Prime Minister Menachem Begin, was an unforgettable experience to say the least.

8 The Making of a Hit

I{\sc t's} Y{\sc our} B{\sc usiness} *changed everything about the Chamber. The program essentially paralleled the advent of Reagan's presidency and was off to a roaring start. In many respects, the show became the chief vehicle in launching the Chamber into the forefront of the national political and business scene—and onto the radar of both major parties.*

At the time the Chamber started the weekly television show, it was still publishing the largest-circulation business magazine, Nation's Business, *plus a newsletter called* The Washington Report, *and was airing a weekly radio program called* What's The Issue?, *on which Lesher appeared and discussed pressing economic topics of the day. It was all part of the organization's fast-growing communications division, designed to get the business perspective out to the country at large—and, specifically, to the lawmakers who set policy. The change in approach was not easy on all of the staff members. Some, who were not part of the communications division, didn't particularly like it when their new boss advised them: "Remember, we are a communications house." They believed that the Chamber was, first and foremost, a policy house.*

"Yes, we are a policy house," Lesher explained. "But we have to communicate with our members to tell them what the question is. They have to communicate back to us to tell us what their answer is. And then we have to communicate with the administration and Capitol Hill. It's all about getting your message out there and having people hear it."

And with It's Your Business *taking off, the Chamber's message was starting to be heard like never before.*

There are so many voices screaming at you for attention that you need all the tools you can muster—and to be able to utilize them effectively if you want to be heard. With that in mind, we poured our time and energy into *It's Your Business*, knowing it was the ideal way to reach our target audience.

To give you a little background, we had already installed a broadcasting satellite atop the Chamber building in order to communicate and hold video-conferences with other Chambers around the country, rallying the troops about legislative issues unfolding in Congress. In addition, we formed the Federation Programs and Services Division, providing interactive business training seminars via satellite, featuring many of the nation's leading experts on quality management.

We focused on teaching business principles and explaining complex issues—akin to a graduate school course. The local chambers could access our satellite feed and sell tickets to these sessions to make some money. We'd also lease our facilities to outside groups, such as the American Medical Association, which used our satellite operation to train doctors in surgical procedures. And we hosted many live videoconferences between the Chamber and government leaders for the United States, Japan, Germany, and Korea. In those days, there was no email or Skype to get the word out en masse, but our electronic technology allowed us to stay connected—and we were truly ahead of the curve in this way.

Now, along came our latest innovation—our own network-style, national issue show, *It's Your Business*—and it was a hit from the start. We scored very high ratings in Washington, where members of Congress watched it routinely because it was always on target with a relevant issue. People in the policy business always watch all of the Sunday morning news talk shows, and in Washington we enjoyed the 12:30 p.m. slot on WMAL-Channel 7—and I have to give a tip of the hat for that to station general manager Tom Cookerly. Broadcasting from a set we constructed in our own building—widely regarded as the most advanced TV studios in town—*It's Your Business* was carried by one hundred fifty stations in markets all over the country, almost equally divided between ABC, CBS, NBC, and independent stations. That was quite an accomplishment for a public affairs show. We never managed to get a decent time slot in New York City—airing at midnight—but for the most part *It's Your Business* enjoyed excellent airtimes and great viewership, with as many as two million people a week watching the show!

This was no vanilla programming operation. While I was exploring the concept of a television show produced by the Chamber, I hired a consultant who had been an expert in communications and public affairs at NASA during my years there. He was emphatic in his belief that debate was a key component of a successful show—something that made total sense to me, appealing to my lifelong penchant for a mixing it up a bit.

From the outset, I insisted that, in order to be taken seriously, *It's Your Business* had to have two representatives from each side of whatever issue was being dissected. That usually meant at least one Democrat and one Republican, perhaps a member of Congress, and a business executive, joined by yours truly to add my perspective. My role required weekly preparation for whatever topic we planned to tackle, but it was well worth the effort—and, for the record, I eventually appeared on all 937 episodes over 18 years (even though my travel for work took me to all fifty states and eighty-five countries in the same period. Thank goodness for video tape!) I will say that I did not take my participation in the show lightly—not for a second. You walk onto the set with a heavy burden of responsibility. You're the president of a large, complicated organization, with a long list of policies to oversee. And you don't want to debate a subject and screw up in the process—whether factually or in terms of policy. On top of that, we had some of the country's most eloquent speakers and leading political, business, and media authorities debating me—and ready to pounce if I made a mistake. That's pressure! At the time, I never thought I was as good as I probably was, but I certainly held my own when the cameras began to roll.

We had a good sense of the show's effectiveness early on, whenever we gave out our Spirit of Enterprise Awards to members of Congress—the honor bestowed to those legislators who voted in line with Chamber policies 70 percent of the time or more on our scorecard. Each year, I'd take my chairman up to the Hill to give out our awards and warn him, "Now you're going to hear two things today. You'll hear that the award is extremely valuable to them for raising money back home, because it reflects the Chamber's approval. Second, they're going to lobby me to be on the TV show. We're paid as lobbyists, but you watch—we'll be lobbied all day long." Sure enough, one congressman after the next would say, "I'd love to be on the show. I haven't been on in a long time. By the way, that show you did two weeks ago, that was my subject—you should have called me."

It's Your Business was a magnet for politicians for a simple reason. You raise money for a politician so he or she can buy time on television. Our show allowed them to skip that step and just go on national television, espousing their positions and showcasing their good work to voters back home, free of charge. Early on, we expanded our studio inside the Chamber building. There was an open courtyard in the building and we filled it in with various offices and the most modern studios in Washington.

The AFL-CIO—the labor organization that took an opposite stance to ours on virtually everything—paid us a compliment while our studio was under construction. The organization's president, Lane Kirkland, who succeeded George Meany, was quoted in the paper saying something to the effect of, "They know what they're doing. They're going into TV and we need to do it, too." The Union folks tried to copy us, but they didn't do it correctly, because they were too concerned with controlling the viewpoints expressed. They booked my chief economist on one of their first shows, but after taping the program they edited out all of his key points. Word got around right away and, consequently, not everyone was willing to appear on the show, and most stations declined to carry it.

When I told my board we were going to do *It's Your Business*, and by the way we planned to book union people, consumer activist Ralph Nader, and others of opposing viewpoints, the reaction I got was: "You're going to do what?" My response was simple—"If you're not going to have a balanced program, you're never going to get stations to carry it."

The reality was this: a balanced format would allow us to barter the show far more effectively to stations, which would have been turned off by a sheer business propaganda show. With a blend of competing perspectives, stations would have greater ability to sell their own commercial time—and we could still run some of our own commercials. Thankfully, August Busch decided he didn't want to spend all of his advertising dollars on beer commercials during NFL telecasts. He also allocated money to create corporate responsibility ads that ran during our show—showcasing what Busch did for the environment and employees. His commitment as a commercial sponsor, buying expensive airtime, made a big difference in helping the show succeed—ultimately helping us offset our formidable production costs.

Furthermore, I stressed to my board that if you really believe in your process, you ought to be willing to put it to the public test. Then, we would take steps to survey reaction to see how viewers reacted to the presentation of points. Sure enough, we found that the audience moved in our direction after they had heard both sides of the argument.

The program, without question, represented one of my biggest achievements in my years at the Chamber—showcasing a topical weekly debate on television and syndicating it ourselves all around the country. We taped the show on Wednesday and transmitted it to stations that same day, leaving space for them to insert their own ads. This form of self-syndication was a win-win—and the product was a winner, too.

In our first year, the moderator was a standout journalist named Karna Small, who had a network news background. She'd grown up in a conservative family that talked politics and issues at the dinner table. Karna did a fine job, but left to join the Reagan administration as deputy press secretary. After an extensive search, we found an ideal replacement—a first-class, award-winning journalist in her own right, Meryl Comer. Meryl would become an institution on the show, eventually serving as moderator for seventeen years, a centerpiece of her Emmy-winning career that made a genuine impact on the Chamber's growth and prowess.

I'm honored by how she remembers the impact we had: "Working on this new show for the Chamber and Dr. Lesher was a unique opportunity and, in my mind, quite a visionary endeavor. In hindsight, there have been a plethora of business news shows, but it was really the first one. And it allowed us to explore the nexus of business and public policy. That truly is a tribute to Dr. Lesher for using the medium in a way that it had not been used before."

We definitely had Washington watching—and dying to participate. A small sampling of guests in our first year alone included economist Alan Greenspan, AFL-CIO director Dr. Rudolph Oswald, such Republicans as Reagan Senior Advisor Pat Buchanan and Senators Ted Stevens of Alaska and Alan Simpson of Wyoming, and Democratic Senators Al Gore of Tennessee and Arizona's Mo Udall. On one show during a commercial break, Senator Diane Feinstein from California leaned over to me and said, "Why is it that all of the business people always sound alike?" I smiled and jabbed back: "Well, we're telling the truth, and we have to say it over and over again for people like you to get it." I don't think she appreciated my humor, but I saw no harm in a little good-natured jousting and I never missed a chance—regardless of a person's political affiliation.

We booked many of the top names in politics and business through the years. There are far too many to mention here, but consider this: over the eighteen years the show operated, more than eighty US senators and three hundred members of the House of Representatives appeared as guests, some more than once. The guest list was like a Who's Who of public affairs. Here is just a very small sample in no particular order: Sen. Tom Foley (D-Wash.), Sen. John Rockefeller (D-W. Va.), Sen. Richard Lugar (R-Indiana), Sen. Bob Dole (R-Kansas), Sen. Tom Eagleton (D-Missouri), Rep. Barney Frank (D-Mass.), Sen. Howard Metzenbaum (D-Ohio), Rep. Barbara Mikulski (D-Md.), Rep. Newt Gingrich (R-Ga.), Rep. Sam Gibbons (D-Fla.), Rep. (and future Vice President) Richard Cheney (R-Wy.), Sen. Lloyd Bentsen (D-Texas), Sen. Arlen Specter (R-Pa.), Sen. Tom Daschle (D-S.D.), Madeleine Albright (then president for the Center of National Policy), and Sen. Trent Lott (R-Miss.)

At least nine guests later ran for president of the United States (Pat Buchanan, Bob Dole, Tom Eagleton, Newt Gingrich, Lindsay Graham, Geraldine Ferraro, Jack Kemp, and Rick Santorum); three were future vice presidents (Joe Biden, Dick Cheney, and Dan Quayle); and three served as majority leaders of the senate (Dole, Mitch McConnell, and Harry Reid). The executive branch was also well represented by various cabinet members (Madeleine Albright and James Baker) as well as key members of the White House staff (David Stockman, Donald Rumsfeld, and Ed Meese).

In addition, we had a marquee list of media members—people like David Gergen of CNN and *U.S. News and World Report*, Hugh Sidey of *Time* magazine, Tom DeFrank of *Newsweek* and Tom Oliphant of the Boston *Globe*. People may not remember that two very familiar commentators on television today got their start as guests on our show: MSNBC's Chris Matthews and CNBC's Larry Kudlow. They were newspaper men and not on television very much until we "discovered" them. We were no different than any other TV production: if a guest came on the show and excelled, we booked that person again. That was the case with Matthews and Kudlow, just as it was with members of Congress, such as Gingrich. Matthews, a former bureau chief for the *San Francisco Examiner* and columnist for the *San Francisco Chronicle,* didn't display the trademark brashness he's known for as host of *Hardball*. He was more laid back, but was still clever and quick, highly articulate, and very personable—and I'm not surprised he's so successful today, whether you agree with him or not.

On occasion, we even reached beyond normal Washington circles, booking such entertainment and sports guests as famed actor E. G. Marshall (who was so nervous he could barely talk, counter to his eloquent acting in film and TV) and "Mr. Cub," Ernie Banks, who weighed in on a show about the economics of baseball.

We talked about every imaginable political and business topic of the day with such topics as: The Way Washington Works, Clean Air, Congressional Politics, From Welfare to Work, Product Liability, Campaign Finance Reform, Illegal Immigration (yes, even back then), a National Lottery, Sports Economics, Nuclear Power, Estate Tax Reform, Education Reform, Eastern Europe, Trade with the Soviets, the Telecommunications Revolution, Clean Water, and many hundreds more.

There was only one topic I refused to include on the show: executive salaries and perks. I would have had to defend them, and I couldn't have justified doing that due to my belief that they were massively out of line—and it's worse than ever today. I've been on many boards and know how the game is played—it's like legalized thievery. The CEO picks his friends for the board and he picks the best of his friends for the compensation committee. The committee proceeds to hire a consultant to compare his or her wage to other CEOs, then calculates some staggering salary figure—justifying it as a way of keeping the CEO from leaving. It was and is utter nonsense, and completely unethical.

As you can tell, *It's Your Business* was a heavyweight show, holding an important place in televised discourse in America. We had the most modern studios in all of Washington and an ace staff in front of the camera and behind the camera. And that prompted us to think about what other programming we could undertake. That led to the addition of a two-hour daily morning program called *First Business* on burgeoning sports cable network, ESPN. *First Business* was a news program that aired at 7:00 a.m. Monday through Friday. The show was geared toward helping small businesses succeed and was carried in a whopping one hundred fifty countries. ESPN catered, in part, to traveling businessmen at the time and our show was a great way to hook that part of the audience. What we learned was that many of them would turn off the hotel TV at night watching sports recaps on ESPN and, when they turned the set back on to start their day, they'd already be tuned in to *First Business*. It was a terrific success, both for us and ESPN.

Bill Grimes, the president of ESPN, visited Agnes and me at our house in Bethesda during that period. We played tennis and basketball and then I invited him to play a round of pool downstairs. He lamented that I suckered him into playing for a little money by playing him left-handed—before I began shooting right-handed and cleaning up. I couldn't resist having a little fun at Bill's expense, with a trick I'd learned years in my Chambersburg youth and later utilized in the army.

Cable was just beginning to take off back then, but I'd see *First Business* on hotel television sets while traveling the world on business. Ted Stevens used to tease me by saying, "Don't you ever move to Alaska, because you could get my seat in a heartbeat. We don't have many channels up here, and your show is on all time!" Between our Sunday syndicated show and daily ESPN offering, we were producing television programming virtually non-stop from Chamber headquarters. In addition to our own telecasts, we rented the studio out—along with our staff to run the operation—to organizations such as the American Medical Association, which used our facilities to broadcast instructional shows on surgical procedures. All of this generated money to help us pay for our own programs.

The general feedback we got from our TV shows was enthusiastic, even though I'll be the first to admit that some of our programs were boring. Face it: making a debate on the minimum wage sound sexy isn't easy. But even with that topic, we managed to create a lively debate—and one that has relevance today as the subject remains a hot-button issue in politics. We'd tackled the topic on several occasions, but in one instance I partnered with the often-controversial mayor of Washington, DC: Marion Barry.

It might have struck viewers as an odd pairing: the head of the famously conservative Chamber of Commerce and an activist Democratic politician. But Barry and I both came down on the same side of the minimum-wage issue: that is to say, *against* raising it. He said, "Look, I've got 18 percent unemployment with black youth right now. If you raise the minimum wage, that'll jump to 35 percent. I want those kids off the street and if they get a job at minimum wage, they'll learn how to do the job, show up on time, and succeed in a work situation. If they do all of that, within six months they'll get a small raise and begin working their way up the ladder."

On the flip side, as Barry and I argued, starting inexperienced workers at an inflated pay rate—exceeding their experience level—could cause complacency among the workers, ultimately make it less likely that they would get ahead, and perhaps make it harder for the businesses to afford keeping them on the payroll. This remains a touchy topic today, because to speak out against raising the minimum wage makes it sound as if you're speaking out against the less advantaged. But that is not the case. The truth is, unions want the minimum wage to go up because that means the price of goods and services increase as well, but that's how you plant the seeds for inflation. Several years before that show with Barry, the Chamber had done a *Nation's Business* interview with Jimmy Carter's brother, Billy—the sensible Carter, as I've explained—and he was absolutely against raising the minimum wage for those same reasons. He said, "I used to have a whole bunch of kids working here. They didn't do much, but I paid them and tried to teach them how to handle a job. But you don't see them anymore—because of the increase in the minimum wage. I can't afford to pay them."

Whatever the topic of the week was, we constantly heard from many viewers who were thrilled that somebody was finally speaking up for business.

What mattered was that *It's Your Business* changed how people looked at the Chamber—from union leaders to K Street lobbyists. On Capitol Hill, the new attitude toward us was underscored by the fact that many politicians were tuning in to the show.

One of the greatest compliments I've been paid about the show came years later from my district's Congressman, Bill Shuster, whose father, Bud, also served in the US House of Representatives and was on *It's Your Business* many times. On a recent trip to Washington, I stopped by Bill's office to introduce myself and he seemed so pleased to meet me. He said, "You're one of the main reasons why I'm where I am today." I asked why, and he explained, "I never missed your show. That's where my interest in government issues developed." I laughed and replied, "Don't give me that—you only watched the show when your dad was on as my partner." But Bill was serious. "I watched your show all the time and was fascinated by all the topics Washington deals with."

To this day, people will still stop me and say they watched me on the show. But the main question I usually get is about Meryl. People will ask, "What was that woman's name?" Everybody wants to know about Meryl because she was so beautiful and so professional. She did that show wonderfully. I'd brief her on the subject each week, because she wasn't trained in economics like I was, and she picked up all the nuances effortlessly. To host that show, you had to have a firm grip on the issues and Meryl always did. And we never had an argument about one thing. I told her, "If you're going to pound on the other side, pound on me, too. Pound on all of us, because the show has to be balanced and it has to be fair."

That's a key reason why so many people watched. My occasional lunch pal, Chief Justice Burger, was a steadfast viewer of the show—and he loved to talk about the issues we dealt with on the program. My friends in the White House certainly were watching too. In fact, our flourishing TV operation caught the attention of one individual in the incoming Reagan administration right away. In January 1981, a week or so after the inauguration, a White House staffer named Charlie Wick made an appointment to see me, accompanied by his wife, Mary Jane, who was Nancy Reagan's best friend. Charlie had been a big band leader in Hollywood, and the Reagans and Wicks had done a lot of socializing over the years. We made small talk and Charlie paid me some compliments about our TV operation. And then he said something that floored me. "Now I'm going to tell you how to do this," he began. "I want the TV operation running twenty-four hours a day, supporting the president."

"What do you mean?" I replied, not even trying to mask my incredulousness.

"I just mean that whatever the president is working on, I want you to support him by covering all of his initiatives—and I want it to be 24/7."

"Well," I answered, keeping my annoyance in check, "understand that we support this President 100 percent. But you can't run a program supporting his initiatives twenty-four hours a day or your audience will shrink to zero. Here's how we do it: we have the news program and tuck in policy issues and stories within that, and we'll get our message out loud and clear."

Charlie and his wife were furious. "I'll tell the president who his real friends are!" he blurted out, as he and his wife left my office in a huff. I thought to myself, "Oh my God. After fighting so much with the Carter people, now I'm going to be fighting with the Reagan folks, too."

Nothing ever came of Charlie's attempt to strong-arm his way into our TV production. He was obviously just a low-level staffer looking for a role for himself, and I'm sure he would have loved nothing more than to attach himself to our operation as a producer, earning brownie points with the president and his senior staff. A few weeks after his visit, I heard that Charlie had been appointed the director of the United States Information Agency, which produces Voice of America. I was never one to hold a grudge so I called him up, congratulated him on the new job, and invited him over to the Chamber for a luncheon, offering to have some of my experts brief him on international issues as we see them.

"You'd do that for me?" he said after a momentary hesitation.

"Absolutely," I answered. "There's a lot of policy in that job that you need to be on top of. "We'll prepare a briefing book for you."

Charlie was so humble and grateful, a completely different person from the man who had tried to muscle his way into our TV operation. He'd been so desperate to assert himself and make an impression on his White House bosses that he'd over-stepped. I had no reason to be vengeful in return. In fact, I believed I was doing the administration a favor by helping Charlie be more effective in his new role. And from what I later heard, he did a good job.

During that first year in office, my dealings with the administration couldn't have been better. Reagan had made good on his promise to end the Iranian hostage crisis that had haunted the Carter administration—with American captives released the day of his inauguration. Next, he set out to deliver on his other fundamental promise: to address the nation's economic woes. He did so with a sweeping tax cut, signing into law the Economic Recovery Act of 1981. The basic premise was that lower taxes would make it easier for struggling citizens to spend more of their hard-earned cash on products or services they desired—thus giving the sagging economy a jolt. At the same time, Reagan aimed to balance the budget with widespread cuts in governmental departments and social programs, while heavily increasing military spending.

The act represented a sharp decrease in marginal income tax rates in the country by 23 percent over three years. Reagan's communication skills served him well as he worked hard to persuade the Congress and country that his approach was needed to escape the grip of a worsening recession. And he relied heavily on the US Chamber of Commerce to support his efforts. Under the banner of "Let's

Rebuild America," the Chamber pulled out all the stops to help get Reagan's program through Congress, and all of us were elated at the outcome, finally having reason to celebrate after our gloomy experience with the Carter White House. I'll always treasure the letter the president sent me in the aftermath, thanking me and the Chamber for our work in helping him get the tax cut approved.

You can imagine why I never anticipated what happened next—a looming tax fight with the president I respected so much, putting my job at the Chamber squarely on the line.

9 Standing My Ground

CRUISING HIGH ABOVE *the clouds somewhere over America, Air Force 1 and Air Force 2 placed more than a few combined phone calls during the summer of 1982 to members of the United States Chamber of Commerce's board of directors. The gist of the airborne messages from President Ronald Reagan and Vice President George Bush was to urge the Chamber to support an unexpected change in course from the commander in chief's heavy tax cut from his first year in office.*

The budget projections that had helped justify the 1981 tax reductions had turned out to be overly rosy. Reagan's budget director, David Stockman, feared that the cuts had been too sharp and would only exacerbate the worst recession in fifty years. With a massive budget deficit for the president to deal with, Stockman believed that it was vital to raise taxes in 1982 by 1.2 percent—generating $150 billion immediately to ease the crisis. The sense of urgency to reverse the initial tax cuts grew deeper amid rising unemployment figures and failing businesses.

The president agreed to a rollback of both corporate tax cuts and individual income tax cuts, amounting to a reversal of about one-third of his 1981 Economic Recovery Act. Now came the hard part—selling the plan to a Congress that had embraced Reagan's campaign promise to cut taxes. The result was frequent and persuasive lobbying from both the president and the vice president to lawmakers and members of the US Chamber. The White House understood the clout that the Chamber had come to wield with Congress and knew the organization could mobilize local chambers throughout the nation to oppose the increase.

That led both Reagan and Bush to place personal calls—even while thirty-five thousand feet above the earth—to Chamber of Commerce leaders. But the organization's president, Dick Lesher, wasn't about to budge. Lesher believed the tax hike was a bad idea, flying in the face of everything the Chamber stood for and so recently had fought for. He and the Chamber board of directors formally opposed the increase. That stance, however, put the Chamber at odds not only with the two most powerful leaders in the country, but eventually placed Lesher in a showdown with a lone yet powerful voice of the Chamber—the chairman himself.

And things were about to get ugly.

There was no doubt about it: Reagan and his team thought that they could not push through the tax increase without the Chamber's backing, resulting in an all-out campaign to get us to change our position.

As background, the Chamber has a longstanding policy of opposing any new taxes or increasing any old taxes—a policy reaffirmed by the board of directors when it decided to oppose Reagan's proposal to raise taxes. As a member of the board myself, I voted against the increase, as did Don Kendall, CEO of Pepsico, Jay Van Andel, CEO of Amway, and many others on the sixty-five-member board. This was intensely difficult to go against a president we held in the highest regard, but we had to stand on principle—regardless of our fondness for Reagan.

This led to calls by the White House from officials who reminded us how much we liked the president and how he felt this was best for the country. But I told them, very respectfully, that our policy dictated that we had to oppose President Reagan. Any change in that position, I explained, would have to come directly from the board itself.

The next thing I knew, the president had called our chairman of the board, Paul Thayer, the president of a large defense contractor called the LTV Corporation, which built airplanes for the military. I wondered how Thayer would handle a high-pressure pitch from the commander in chief himself, and hoped he would stand his ground.

Thayer was a decorated World War II aviation hero with the US Navy, earning a "flying ace" status in an F4F Wildcat, a man who clearly relished attention. He had a penchant for the limelight, flying his fighter and leading his squadron underneath the Golden Gate Bridge in showboat style when he returned from combat in the Pacific, where he was credited with numerous air victories and sinking a Japanese destroyer. He was accustomed to winning high-pressure fights. After the war, Thayer worked as airline transport pilot, a chief test pilot, and eventually president of Ling-Temco-Vought, better known as LTV. Eventually rising to the company's CEO, Thayer turned around LTV's sagging fortunes and was on a path to becoming Chairman of the US Chamber.

Thayer and I got along very well, though there was always a natural competition between the Chamber president—a position with no set term limit—and the chairman of the board, who serves for two years—one as chairman, one as vice chairman—in representing the board at large. I can tell you I wasn't happy to learn that Thayer had once purposely rolled his corporate jet with a member of my staff in the plane holding a Pepsi—he wanted to demonstrate that he could roll it so fast that the drink wouldn't spill. Neither my staffer nor I appreciated that stunt.

In some ways, Thayer had a larger-than-life mystique—a man who was said to have crashed six planes in his life and walked away unharmed from all of them. He was obviously well aware of my opposition—and that of the Chamber board—to Reagan's plan to raise taxes. Then came the aforementioned call from the president, who invited Thayer to lunch so they could discuss the new tax-raising initiative. Thayer immediately accepted—no doubt flattered by the personal invitation. When the day arrived for his appointment at the White House, Thayer popped his head inside my office to tell me he'd let me know how it went.

"Now you know what this is about, don't you?" I said, looking him straight in the eyes. "You're going to have a one-on-one meeting with the president. And he's going to twist your arm to get Chamber support for the tax bill."

"Aw, Dick, don't worry about me," I recall him replying. "I'm more opposed to that tax bill than you are."

With that, Thayer departed and I went back to work in my office, which has a wonderful view across the park of the White House. This is significant because it was always possible to see a flock of reporters standing by White House entrance, waiting to interview anyone leaving. My longtime Chamber counsel, Larry Kraus, has a vivid memory of what happened next.

"Sure enough, all these reporters were waiting to interview Paul Thayer as he left his meeting with President Reagan," Larry recollects. "They asked what was discussed and Paul explained that the president asked for our support on the tax increase. One reporter asked what Thayer told him and he responded, 'I told him that the Chamber would support the increase in taxes.'

The next thing I knew, Thayer was striding into my office and telling me bluntly, "Put out a press release that we support the president."

I remember actually laughing at the statement, then remarking, "You're kidding, right?"

"No, dammit, I'm not kidding. I gave him my word that we'd support him on this."

"Well," I responded, "you made a promise that you can't deliver."

Suddenly, Thayer's firm tone turned to bluster. "What do you mean?" he shot back. "I'm the CEO of this organization and I will tell you how to run it."

"No," I countered. "You're *not* the CEO."

"Well, who the hell is then? It's certainly not *you*."

I paused for a moment, and calmly played a card I knew I had all along. "Well, the founding fathers of this organization were smart enough to foresee a problem like this possibly arising, so they made the *board* the CEO."

"What do you mean?" Thayer interjected, clearly unsure of the fine points of our power structure.

"What I mean." I said matter-of-factly, "is if you want to deliver your promise to Reagan, you're going to have to call a board meeting and convince the board to change its position. If they don't, then you're going to have to eat some crow and apologize to the president."

By now, Thayer was red-faced and screaming at me, promising that he would have my job. The stage was set for a confrontation I thought I should win, though anything could happen. There was no way to predict the outcome of such a combustible situation—with a strong-willed chairman pushing hard for his position, appealing to board members to support a president we all respected. In spite of our clear difference with him on this matter, he could emerge the winner.

If I lost, and the board voted to side with Thayer, it could cost me my job. Regardless of the potential outcome, I'd never run from a fight in my life, and my firm belief was that we should oppose the tax increase—unless the board decided otherwise.

A board meeting was held several days later. I would guess 90 percent of the members were in attendance, and everyone in the room knew what was happening. Even prior to the meeting, board members had apparently been dividing into two opposing camps. Of course, I had people in each of those camps privately letting me know what was transpiring. That's how I learned Thayer's strategy: he would come to the meeting and state that the White House would not work with the Chamber any longer as long as I was president.

Armed with that inside knowledge, we got on the phone with top administration officials at the Western White House, Reagan's Rancho del Cielo home in California, where the president was at the time. Our vice chairman, a good friend of mine named Ed Dodd, the CEO of Owens-Illinois, spoke with Reagan's acting chief of staff, Craig Fuller. And Fuller's reply was something to this effect: "Let me assure you that tactic will never work, because while we might disagree with Dick once in a while, we respect him and we respect the Chamber's right to have your own position."

The next day, there was a palpable air of tension when the debate finally began in the Chamber boardroom. It was a closed-door session and the only staff people allowed inside were me, my general counsel, Larry Kraus, and a stenographer to keep a record of what was said. Thayer stood up to initiate the proceedings, ready to go on the attack, but before he could begin his argument, Dodd interrupted: "I make a motion on the by-laws that you cannot conduct this meeting because you have a personal interest in it. You must step down and let the vice chairman conduct the meeting."

The room was immediately abuzz at the surprise move, but there was no arguing the point—it was in the rules, and we knew that Thayer likely had no knowledge of that stipulation. It was an excellent tactic, throwing Thayer off his game.

"Well, I'm not stepping down unless *Lesher* does," Thayer blurted out.

I'd been sitting in my normal seat at the head table and—without missing a beat—I gathered up my notebook and took a seat in a chair on the floor. "Come on, Paul," I said. "Let's sit down and let them hammer it out."

Thayer had no choice but to take his seat as well and let the proceedings continue. When his turn came, Thayer stood and made his impassioned speech about the need to support the president—and then launched what he thought was his heavy ammunition: that the White House said it would no longer work with the Chamber so long as I was president.

When Thayer was finished, Dodd spoke up. "I'm sorry if you believe that, but you're dead wrong."

"What do you mean?" Thayer challenged.

"Well, I happened to talk to the White House last night about that very subject, and they said 'We're not going to make this personal. We just want the Chamber to support us—it has nothing to do with Dick Lesher.'"

The debate continued briefly after that, but there was little doubt that we had depleted the firepower of the old fighter pilot. Finally, the matter came to a vote, and the Chamber board reaffirmed its position to oppose the tax increase. Then, as Larry recalls, there was a second matter to decide:

"They took a vote on whether to replace Dick—and nobody wanted him to go. One of Dick's strong traits is his belief in ethical behavior—you stand up for your principles. He brought that in from day one. Dick stood up for the Chamber policy and his own beliefs on the issue, even though he thought the world of Ronald Reagan. It's a great example of what makes Dick the person he is."

It was a major victory and one that I fully savored—not because it caused Thayer deep embarrassment, which you better believe it did, but because I felt it was critically important to stand on principle with such a key issue at stake.

The fact is, I was closer to Reagan than any other president during my twenty-two-year tenure. We enjoyed each other's company, which is precisely what made it difficult to find each other on opposite sides of the fence on a matter so important to him.

In that regard, I'll always feel gratified by something former senator and one-time presidential candidate Bob Dole said while in Chambersburg years later to campaign for a local candidate. I went out to the rally to see him and hear him speak. Before he started with his remarks, he told the crowd, "I see my good friend Dick Lesher in the audience. I just visited with him. I know he's Chambersburg's favorite son, and I want you to know that Dick ran the US Chamber of Commerce for many years with great integrity." Those two words meant—and continue to mean—so much to me. People like Bob Dole don't say that about just anybody in Washington, and I always strived to live up to that standard.

When I first arrived at the Chamber, in fact, I sat with my officers early on and laid down the ground rules for how we would operate. I said, "Now look, there are a couple of things that are not negotiable. We are going to operate with integrity and go by the numbers. We're not going to cheat on anything. If you travel, the Chamber will reimburse your expenses. But don't *ever* pad them—that's the quickest way to get in trouble. I learned that from James Webb at NASA. When we flew on NASA's main jet and the bar opened, all the liquor was paid for out of Webb's pocket—he was that careful about never getting any perks or even allowing for the appearance of it. When Congress pressed him on what kind of limousines he relied on for coming and going around town, he had a ready answer: a Checker cab. The truth was, that vehicle was spacious and comfortable on the inside, but it was still an ugly old cab on the outside. Webb simply never gave opponents any ammunition to attack him with—and it was a smart way to operate.

During that same period, I told my staff, "Mark my words. We're going to be audited by the IRS in the next five years." If you were at all boisterous—and we certainly were changing the way we did business—the IRS would come and see you and very likely audit your books. Sure enough, several years later, the IRS did decide to audit us and even moved an auditor into our building to go through all our files with meticulous precision. He spent weeks there. And finally, on one Friday afternoon, he told Larry Kraus that he would propose charging the Chamber with some minor infraction. Larry looked at him and starting laughing. He said, "After all the work you did, you're going to do that to us? I want to see you try." On Monday, the auditor came in and sheepishly retracted his plan to charge us with any penalty—there was absolutely nothing we had done wrong.

These were enormously busy times, and I got a chuckle one day when I received a letter from a former management professor at Indiana. "You've come a long way from that night watchman's job at Ralph Rogers Construction Company." I guess I had made a lasting impression with the IU faculty for my supercharged work habits. At least I was getting regular sleep now, but my schedule was about as packed as you could imagine. I utilized a driver to get me to and from the Chamber from the suburbs of Maryland to downtown Washington at 1614 H. Street, N.W., because doing so allowed me to read and work from the time I got in the car—on the way to the office or home. It was an expense I could easily justify given the constant and multiple demands on my time and it served me well. But I was never one for frivolous and showy travel in fancy limos, and I was very careful about how we spent our money—making certain we never borrowed, took on debt, or had a mortgage on our building.

And I was never one to play politics with positions, such as when Paul Thayer demanded we support the president, even though some might have seen it as the expedient course of action. I should add—in spite of my resistance and the backing from my board—that Reagan's tax increase eventually passed, signed into law as the Tax Equity and Fiscal Responsibility Act of 1982.

In essence, Congressional Democrats agreed to cut three dollars in spending for every one dollar raised in taxes—a compromise that amounted to a three-year total of a $380 billion reduction in budget deficits. (Dole, then Chairman of the Senate Finance Committee and eventual Majority Leader, led the Senate fight to approve the increase over objections from Democrats.) And there's one other note, literally—the one I received on White House stationary from President Reagan, following a letter I'd sent congratulating him on passage of the bill. It read:

Dear Dick:

Thanks for your letter of congratulations on the tax bill. Passage was certainly a challenge, and I missed having the Chamber officially on our side.

I understand why the Chamber could not support this legislation as an institution, and I respect your opposition to tax increases. As you are aware, I am also philosophically against increasing taxes, and it was not without some difficulty that I ultimately decided to support this legislation.

I, too, look forward to our working together again to keep the Federal Government living within its means through a focus on decreased spending rather than increased taxes.

I trust that you will continue to work with Elizabeth Dole and her staff on these and other issues of mutual concern.

With best wishes,

Sincerely,

Ronald Reagan

One additional thought on Thayer is in order. He was quite disgruntled after the messy showdown and there was no way he could remain effective in his position. Consequently, we helped get him a job as deputy secretary of defense in 1983—a job at the Pentagon we knew he would enjoy due to his stellar military service, especially since he was ready to retire from LTV.

But Thayer was only on the job for a year when the government brought charges against him for insider trading. He was sentenced to four years in a minimum-security prison for obstructing justice in the investigation.

While in prison, he wrote a form letter to all the many people who'd written letters on his behalf asking for clemency. He thanked them for their help, and added that he didn't find the surroundings bad. He described how he took Toastmasters class one night a week, Spanish lessons on another night, and could work out every day. The most amazing thing, he continued, was the high caliber of talent behind bars with him. His kicker went something like this: "I could run any company in America with this talent."

It was a decidedly surreal conclusion to a challenging episode, but one that ultimately fortified the Chamber's stature as a force on the political and business scene in America. And, in some respects, we were only just getting started.

* * *

Soon after I took over the Chamber, we received a proposal from the NAM, the National Association of Manufacturers about merging with our organization. NAM's chairman at the time was the vice chairman of US Steel, and in hindsight, it's clear that what he was trying to do was gain control over both the Chamber and NAM. We convened a meeting to consider the idea, and my board made it clear that the number one condition would be that I would run the combined organization, otherwise the discussion was over.

The NAM people immediately affirmed that they wanted me to serve as the overall leader, so our talks proceeded for several months. Meanwhile, I met with the head of the Business Round Table, John Harper—whose group included many of the country's largest corporations—and set in motion a plan to bring his organization into the merger, keeping the company intact but managing its staff work. Harper, who was a good friend, committed to the plan. It was all set to go. But NAM. balked, making it clear the company's leadership had intended to put its CEO in charge all along. My board told them to take a hike, and that was the end of what would have resulted in a far larger, more powerful, version of the US Chamber.

I certainly have no regrets about that and was more than busy with the work we already had on our plate. I even found time to pen the first of two books, entitled *Economic Progress . . . It's Everybody's Business.* Published by the US Chamber, I was particularly proud of the foreword, written by the thirty-eighth president of the United States, Gerald R. Ford, whose words still mean a great deal to me:

> Dr. Lesher is a thoroughly educated man, having earned a doctorate in business administration while simultaneously matriculating at the school of hard knocks—he held down two jobs to put himself through school. His background is one reason why he is as much at ease discussing economics and exports with presidents and prime ministers as he is talking about take-home pay and taxes with keypunch operators and small business people.
>
> Through it all, he has acquired a devotion to the principles of free market economics that can be best measured by his enthusiasm when he describes how those principles can be successfully applied or by his alarm when he considered how rapidly they are being thrown away in America.

I will share just a small sample of my introduction in the book, because I believe the sentiments remain as true today as they did when I wrote this, five years into my job as the Chamber's president. "Winston Churchill once said: 'Some see private enterprise as a predatory target to be shot, others as a cow to be milked, but few are those who see it as a sturdy horse pulling the wagon.' If we are to surmount the problems challenging America in the 1980s—problems which seem to grow more difficult and dangerous by the day—we must begin rebuilding the nation's economic base by harnessing the tremendous, neglected potential of the private enterprise system."

My absolute faith in the private enterprise system—in business as a driving force in America's greatness—influenced everything the Chamber took on. And as Reagan suggested in his letter to me, we would indeed continue to work together in our shared vision for rebuilding America and power of free enterprise. On various occasions, he would visit our TV studio to tape messages, rather than utilizing government studios. If the purpose of the commercial had anything to do with campaigning for someone or a political issue—or even if the spot could be construed as politically based, thus violating campaign restrictions—the president would use our studios for a small rental fee.

If I knew the president was coming over, I'd stop down to watch the taping and shoot the breeze in the green room while he was waiting to speak his lines. It was fun to watch. Reagan would come in, tell a joke or two, have his make-up applied, and then receive the script literally moments before it was time to go on camera. He'd say, "Let me see if I can go out and get this right the first time."

Then, he'd walk onto the set, sit down, adjust his microphone and—as soon as the cameras rolled—knock it out like he'd been practicing for a week. By contrast, when Vice President Bush came over, he usually had to do multiple takes. He seldom got it right the first time. Members of his staff, watching the taping, had to decide which of them would have to suggest to him he needed to do the shot over. Then again, when the president picked up the mic, nobody I ever saw had the same smoothness and ability to absorb lines and read them completely naturally—on the first try. Reagan was a master of that.

I enjoyed great access with Reagan and his team. I remember one breakfast we had with him and his secretary of defense, Caspar Weinberger, in the White House dining room. A half a dozen CEOs of defense and space contractors were there, suggesting to the president that if he eliminated a lot of paperwork and redundancy, the government could save billions of dollars. Reagan looked at Weinberger and asked, "Is that true?" Cap said, "I don't know. We'll look into it." Of course, that never happened. But our purpose was to urge the administration to do something about spending, and that remains the downfall of conservatives—too much spending. Reagan, to his credit, was at least receptive to our message but Weinberger apparently had more important things to do.

Amid such serious discussions, Reagan proved to be a connoisseur of jokes, a connection we continued to share throughout his presidency. He got a big kick out of one joke—actually a true story—I told him about Daniel Webster's desk. The Chamber building sits on the site where Webster's home once stood. We had his famous desk in our library and it needed repairs. So we finally sent it out for refinishing and, when the truck driver brought it back, he said to the receptionist, "Would you call upstairs and tell Mr. Webster his desk is ready." Reagan threw back his head, laughing heartily. I also had an arsenal of lawyer jokes that Reagan appreciated—he always wanted to hear my latest. But one of my all-time favorites had nothing to do with attorneys, and it soon became a favorite of his as well, even taking on a life of its own inside the White House.

One of our excellent writers at the Chamber, Ben Elliot, who worked with me on my weekly *Voice of Business* column and many other projects, wound up as

Reagan's number one economics and business speechwriter. I would call Ben up every once-in-a-while to congratulate him on a speech that underscored Chamber policy, and one day he inserted one of my jokes into a presidential speech.

Here's how it goes: There were two young brothers—one an extreme optimist and one an extreme pessimist. They put them in separate rooms—with the optimistic brother going into a room full of manure, the pessimistic brother in a room full of new toys.

A little while later, they asked the pessimist, "Why aren't you playing with these toys? He said, "I just know if I touch one, I'd break it and I'd be in trouble." Then they went down the hall and looked in on the optimist and there he was, digging enthusiastically through the manure. "What are you *doing*?" they asked.

"I just know with all this manure," he explained, "there *has* to be a pony in here somewhere!"

Reagan used that joke in a speech he gave in Mexico and they just loved it. The punch line even became a buzzword in the White House, I was later told. When a problem would arise, someone would pipe up and say, "Look for the pony."

* * *

Laughter was an essential way to break up the tension in the high-pressure world of Washington and national politics. So much of what demanded my attention was serious business—all in the name of strengthening the hand of business.

One of the sources of that strength was my board of directors—an all-star collection of corporate business leaders that truly made people sit up and take notice of the Chamber. Before I'd arrived, the board included many second-tier executives who didn't even represent their industry or speak authoritatively for their companies. I knew that wouldn't work if I was to build an organization that had teeth and could truly pave the way for change.

My solution was to bring over CEOs from my previous organization, the National Center for Resource Recovery, creating a very powerful board of directors that gave the Chamber clout and credibility for the first time. We had people such as Don Kendall, CEO of Pepsi, August Busch III and CEO of Anheuser-Busch, on down the line. This new-look board of directors sent a message that these people and their companies cared about what was going on at the Chamber.

On Capitol Hill, the expertise and vitality of the Chamber commanded ever-growing respect from congressional committees, which frequently sought out members of our staff for advice and insight on key issues of the day. In addition, we succeeded in building effective coalitions of business organizations to present a united front before policymakers. The work kept me extremely busy, but I enjoyed every minute of it—a mixture of management, speech-making, travel, occasionally testifying on the Hill, constant one-on-one meetings in the House and Senate, frequent meetings with executive branch officials, cabinet members and sub-cabinet officers—and I still managed to play golf on Sunday mornings!

We certainly were energized by the strides we were making, and one indication of progress was the newfound attention we received from politicians. I remember how North Carolina senator Jesse Helms became such a big fan of ours that he invited me to his office on various occasions—always contriving a media opportunity around my visit. I'd walk in and a member of the print or electronic press just "happened" to call in while I was there, and he'd tell the reporter, "Oh, let me put the head of the Chamber, Dick Lesher, on the phone with you." He wanted me to extoll his pro-business voting record to get some positive coverage back home. Things like that truly illustrated the power of the Chamber.

Naturally, we worked as hard as ever to get Reagan reelected in 1984, though as it turned out, he didn't need much of a helping hand. His landslide victory over Democratic candidate Walter Mondale, capturing 58.8 percent of the popular vote and winning the electoral vote 525-13, was a massive mandate—building on his 1980 showing against Carter when he won the electoral vote 489–49 and the popular vote with 50.8 percent. I'd like to think that Reagan and the US Chamber were both coming of age. Contrary to many reports in the media, I found that he was still at the top of his game in his second term. The press often tried to paint Reagan as a president lacking in intelligence, and now hinted that he had early-onset Alzheimer's in his second term. That's simply nonsense.

He was smart, fun-loving—and, at times, reserved—and very much in control of things from day one until he left office. I'm happy to say that he even shared some of the jellybeans he kept in the Oval Office with me, and I've saved a few for posterity. All the while, he never lost his taste for jokes—only the topic changed from lawyers to Russia. This was due, of course, to all the attention focused on the Soviet Union, punctuated in 1987 by his famous Berlin Wall exhortation to President Mikhail Gorbachev to "tear down this wall."

When I look back, I feel so fortunate to have overlapped Reagan's presidency, at such a critical point in the nation's history and for the US Chamber of Commerce. We had the same goals—both domestically for our economy, with our mission dovetailing neatly with his; and internationally, with the Berlin Wall beginning to collapse, opening major new avenues to free enterprise. The Chamber had been hoping that would happen for years, and Reagan paved the way for its eventual demise in 1989, a year after he left office. I'm forever proud of a memento I was given after the Berlin Wall fell—a plaque that contains a piece of the wall. There are only two such plaques in existence. One was presented to President George H. W. Bush, the other to me by the Hungarian government. I had made two trips to that country giving my speech about free enterprise—just as I had done in countries such as Taiwan, Poland, and throughout Latin America.

At a core level, the Reagan years tapped my own feelings about the power of the economic system we have in this country. I have a deep faith in our system. I believe it is what makes America great—a message I shared as much as I could during my years running the Chamber, at home and abroad. In pages to come later in this book, I will delve further into my desire and efforts to spread these convictions in other countries, where basic freedoms had long been suppressed.

For now, I reflect with gratitude on the relationship I was fortunate to enjoy with one of our country's great presidents—made even stronger, ironically, by a disagreement on principle that shaped both of our tenures.

10 Crusader for Capitalism

THE MODERNIZED, EMPOWERED *Chamber of Commerce was well established by the time George Bush took office in 1989. But rather than stand pat, Dick Lesher continued to build on the organization's success by orchestrating more innovation and change in the way the Chamber did business—all the way through his retirement in 1997 during the Democratic presidential administration of Bill Clinton.*

Bush retained many key players from Reagan's White House, the most important one being chief of staff Jim Baker. And the new president's programs essentially built on Reagan's domestic and foreign initiatives.

At the conclusion of the first year of his term, Bush invited a group of trusted advisors to the Oval Office to sit around a table and reflect on the past twelve months, which included the historic end of the Berlin Wall and the anti-Communist revolution in Czechoslovakia, coupled with China's repressive squashing of student-led protests in Tiananmen Square.

Lesher was among the elite group of invitees. True to his pull-no-punches form, the Chamber leader, now in his fifteenth year on the job, offered an assessment wrapped in directness and humor.

"When we go out into the next century and look back at this year, it will be remembered as the period when the whole world discovered that communism and socialism did not work. The whole world except China, Cuba . . . and Congress."

The room—filled with Bush and his senior White House aides, along with heads of various organizations—burst into laughter as Lesher continued. "I'm just trying to make the point that we should know by now that big government doesn't work. But as we sit here, there are dozens of bills on Capitol Hill proposing a bigger role for government." It was a point he wanted to underscore to the Bush administration and, on occasion, to the Reagan administration: that not enough was being done to reduce the size and reach of government—a core belief of Lesher's own administration.

In spite of that frustration, the Chamber continued to score an array of victories through the early-to-mid-1990s. It successfully pushed for comprehensive reform of US trade law to provide business with heightened competitive stature, playing a role in the reestablishment of the General Agreement on Tariffs and Trades (GATT), and the enactment of the North American Free Trade Agreement (NAFTA) with both deals designed to boost US exports and job growth. Lesher supported Clinton on passage of NAFTA, receiving a personal note from the president that read, in part: "Dear Dick, I am deeply grateful for your support for my admin-istration's efforts to pass the historic North American Free Trade Agreement."

Addressing a national crisis in education, the Chamber created the Center for Workforce Preparation, endeavoring to help state and local chambers of commerce identify and implement education reform with the aim of building a stronger work force. And it released a software tool, In$ite, to help school districts track how their finances are spent.

During the full twenty-two years of Lesher's tenure, countless foreign heads of state and dignitaries from all over the world visited the Chamber, bolstering improved economic relations with the United States and bringing increased cred-ibility to the once-staid organization. A "Spirit of Enterprise Fund" raised money to modernize Chamber headquarters, while keeping the organization debt-free.

Meanwhile, the Chamber burgeoned in size from fifty-two thousand in 1975, the year Lesher took over, to more than two hundred thousand members in the 1990s—a clear reflection of the boundless energy, clear vision, and winning per-sonal style he brought to the position.

Yet of all his accomplishments, none gave him greater satisfaction than the opportunity to spread overseas his central belief in the power of the free enterprise system—especially to students in China and Czechoslovakia eager to learn more about democracy. The visits he paid to those countries in the 1980s—and the gospel he spread at critical points in their social and economic history—warrant further examination as defining moments in his legacy.

The history of industry is competition. And when a new idea comes along—whether it's beer manufacturing or automobiles—a multitude of companies spring up out of the woodwork to bring their products to market. Eventually, there are too many of them and the lesser ones lose money and fall by the way-side. If you look back in time one hundred fifty years, we had about one hundred fifty brewers in America. Five years ago, there were about six that were profitable and all the rest had disappeared. The same pattern also holds true of automobiles and any number of other industries. Consolidation is simply a normal part of the competitive, free-market process.

Guiding any successful business are three basic documents: a balance sheet, a budget, and a P&L statement, short for profit and loss. Productive companies program for losses, because there is always a certain risk involved when you start a business. Some of those risks are evident from the outset and never disappear, some spring up unexpectedly. Yet that inherent aspect of risk and reward lies at the heart of our system and helps it to thrive. And that's part of the message I tried to teach when I was overseas.

My first Chamber trip to China came in 1979 when the country was just starting to crack open the door to new ideas from the West. Nixon had gone there in the early 1970s, a bold move that laid the groundwork for improved relations and served as a catalyst for change in helping China to broaden its outlook. But this was a slow process and by the late 1970s, very few American business representatives had followed Nixon's lead.

I very much wanted to travel to China to see what I could do to nurture a relationship on behalf of American business. Many companies wanted to create a presence in the previously closed, super power nation, which was poised to become the world's largest market. And I hoped to establish the roots for an American Chamber office in Beijing.

Bear in mind, my foreign trips on behalf of the Chamber—whether to Europe, Asia, the Middle East, Africa, or South America—weren't simply for show, involving a handshake, show-and-tell and out the door. They were substantive, working meetings to try to further privatization of government entities, boost the effectiveness of the American Chambers of Commerce located in the respective countries, and build free-enterprise bridges between the two countries. Governments talk to each other all the time, but what I wanted to demonstrate was interest from the private sector—and underscore that American companies wanted to come there, live and work there, and engage in trade and investment. That was the umbrella under which all of my travel to foreign nations took place.

My overseas outreaches coincided with the creation of CIPE, the Center for International Private Enterprise. The Reagan administration had advocated for a law that Congress passed—designating the AFL-CIO and the Chamber as recipients for funds to teach democracy around the world. Essentially, CIPE built on the mission the Chamber and I had already undertaken in this regard. The organization has been doing phenomenal work in its quarter century of existence—teaching countries how to organize an association that can influence public policy. I bring this up as a shining example of how congressional action worked beautifully, unlike the many boondoggles that have been created by well-intentioned laws. I was so pleased with CIPE, which was established as a separate entity within the Chamber, an extension of the National Endowment for Democracy. From the start, the organization received and funded many proposals for conferences, publications, and studies all over the developing world. And it paralleled my personal commitment to spreading the virtues of free enterprise around the world, as with my travel to China.

My impression of China in 1979 was that it was completely backward. I think there were only one hundred thousand automobiles in the entire country. All you saw, on every street, were people on bicycles. To get around, we were chauffeured in military cars. The country was completely owned and operated by the restrictive government. During the visit, I had one hole in my calendar and I asked for permission to speak with students. Revolutions are most often led by the young—older people fear change and disorder. And I relished the idea of engaging young minds in a frank exchange about the benefits of a free economy, though my hosts weren't certain they were going to permit me to meet with them.

Then, in the midst of my stay, I was informed that I would indeed be addressing a group of students the next day. I'm not sure that talking openly about the virtues of free enterprise in a rigid, authoritarian country was the safest choice I could have made. It was highly possible that my trip could have been abruptly curtailed had my hosts objected to the tenor of my comments. But I was determined to speak from the heart and let the chips fall where they may.

When I arrived at a hall to give my talk, the large group seated in front of me didn't look like students at all, and it turns out they weren't. The gathering consisted primarily of government people, but I still was being given the opportunity to deliver my speech on the practical benefits of capitalism over communism. During my introduction to the group, the presenter said something along the lines of, "America is rich. China is poor. You must help us, so we are glad you are here."

In my opening remarks, I played off the introduction. "China is not poor," I began. "China is rich. You kept your oil in the ground until the price went up." The line caused laughter to ripple through the room, breaking the ice. "But I'm serious," I continued. "You are a country rich with resources, home to the most inventive population in the history of the world, and yet you are stagnant. Why is that? I believe it is because of your economic system. You don't believe in incentives and rewards for people who are more productive, which means they don't get anything more than the people who are not productive."

If you give everybody the same pay, I stressed, then everyone will work at the same low level without any motivation to excel further. But with an incentive system, those who are more ambitious and have more to offer will climb the ladder. This, I explained, was the power of capitalism. The world lived in poverty throughout most of history. And it was only because of capitalism that emerged two hundred–plus years ago, primarily in the United States, that real economic growth took root.

I went on to talk specifically about the role of profits, private property and ownership, and re-emphasized the part played by incentives to galvanize the economy and create productivity. My lecture was greeted with enthusiastic applause. Unbeknownst to me, one member of the audience was the deputy director of national economic planning for the entire country.

In appearance, she was a little old lady, but she wielded a great deal of clout. Later that day, I was informed by a translator that my schedule had been changed because the deputy director enjoyed my talk so much that she wanted me to address her staff the next morning. I was delighted and proceeded to give a talk on the benefits of capitalism and a competitive, free-market economy. I would dearly love to know the long-range impact of my speech about profits and loss and individual incentives.

In my view, that talk—against the backdrop of where China was economically and where it was heading in the next ten years—had to have made some impact on spurring the country's move toward Westernization. There's obviously no way to trace the effect of my words, but consider what China was like in 1979. Workers were not even allowed to change jobs. Positions were assigned to them by the system.

I'd spent time in a factory where workers were grinding jade and coral and turning out what I call instant artifacts. I spoke with an old man of about seventy-five or eighty who was sitting on a bench and using a pneumatic drill, working on creating a small replica of a sailing ship. I asked him how long he'd been doing that. At first, they thought I meant how long he had been working on the ship. "Two years," the interpreter answered. I clarified what I meant: "No, no—how long has he worked at that trade in this factory?" The interpreter asked the old man, and then came an answer that amazed me: "He was assigned this job in the seventh grade."

Those words truly had an impact on me—the idea of a worker being assigned a job as a child and holding it well into his or her senior years. As I traveled through China the rest of the trip, I started asking that question when I encountered other workers. And the answer I received from everyone was the same. People were assigned their jobs, and worked very hard at them for a lifetime out of fear of losing their position completely.

That fact ran sharply counter to a key tenet of capitalist economy—the mobility of labor, which is essential to driving an economy. The principle also applies to the transfer of technology—the concept that was central to my years at NASA. Think about it this way: if I hire you and you're a good engineer or inventor, you automatically bring those assets to my company. That's simply a form of technology transfer, and a reason why mobility of labor is extremely important from a corporate perspective—as well as an individual's viewpoint. Any person should have the right to switch jobs if they are unhappy with the one they are in. Yet that was an impossibility in China at that time.

Now, flash forward ten years to my second trip to the country, in March 1989. I very much wanted to return in an attempt to foster a stronger relationship with the Chinese government—one that would help open the door to increased economic freedom at a time when the world's most populous nation appeared to be approaching a crossroads. But the trip served a potentially greater purpose as well.

We had heard reports that Chinese Premier Li Peng was considering pulling back on the progressive steps of the previous decade. After allowing citizens to have more freedom of choice economically, he had grown concerned about China's increasing inflation. Peng's waffling about official policies worried business interests in the United States and certainly drew the attention of the US Chamber of Commerce. My trip would include a personal meeting with him to discuss China's direction, encouraging him to maintain the current economic freedoms.

When I touched down, I could see immediately that a profound change had taken place in the ten years between trips. Highways were under construction to accommodate all the vehicles that citizens now owned and operated. There were signs of affluence, as well as typical big-city sights of people selling neckties, scarves, and goods on street corners—something that hadn't even been permitted when I had last seen China. Others were even starting their own businesses. I met with fifteen company chiefs, all of whom had launched their operations in the past decade. The whole country seemed to be waking up to the idea of private enterprise. And it struck me that my words from 1979—about the importance of mobility of capital and the mobility of people—might have spurred some of the economic progress I was witnessing now.

One afternoon, I sat in a meeting room filled with entrepreneurs and asked a woman in attendance what she wanted to do. "I want to become the richest woman in China," she replied unabashedly. I asked her how she planned to do that and she responded that she intended to build a string of hotels. When I inquired how many she already had, her words surprised me. She already owned two. "Our family house was large," she said, "so we started to rent rooms, got some income, and we bought another." I sat in complete amazement, listening to these aspiring entrepreneurs—now living in an entirely new atmosphere that gave them the freedom to chart their own courses.

Then came the meeting with Premier Peng that I'd looked forward to with great anticipation. Over the course of an hour, with videotape rolling to capture the session, we each made our case, debating what future course would benefit China the most. I urged him not to curtail all the positive steps that had taken place to create a more vibrant economy in his country. Finally, I remarked, "If you reinstitute controls, Premier Peng, you will have riots in the streets." Through his interpreter, he responded, "No, I believe that if I *don't* reinstitute controls, we will have rioting in the streets due to inflation." It was not the response I hoped for.

Later that same week, I was allowed to address a gathering of genuine students, not a crowd of government workers as had been the case in my first talk. I remember that the auditorium was built to accommodate some three hundred people, but when I walked on stage with the president of the university, it appeared that five hundred students were crowded into every available inch of space, sitting in chairs, and standing along the walls and in the back of the room.

They all spoke English and I could sense the frustration with China's leadership. At the same time, they were so excited to hear an official from the United States talk about free enterprise and freedom in general. I think if I'd have asked them to burn down Beijing, they would have—the situation was becoming that volatile.

One month later, Peng indeed followed through on the course of action we all had feared, reinstituting economic and political controls in China. And on April 15, 1989, the infamous Tiananmen Square protests began, with Chinese students demonstrating in Beijing against Peng's decision. It was estimated that as many as a million people, mostly students, occupied the square during the seven-week protest, in a concerted effort to send their pro-reform message to the world.

The episode finally reached a head on June 4, when the government, under the leadership of Deng Ziaoping, turned on the unarmed crowds with armed troops and tanks, resulting in a death toll estimated from the hundreds to the thousands. The crackdown included a wave of arrests around the country of protesters and sympathizers. Foreign journalists documenting the unrest were kicked out of China to curtail coverage of the violence, while the incremental economic and political progress that had been made over the prior decade screeched to a halt.

It was shocking and somewhat surreal to learn of these events, having been so encouraged by the steps forward China had been taking since my 1979 visit. My feelings were further amplified by the fact that I had met with Li Peng on the eve of the Tiananmen Square protest, then saw the outcome of his actions—the chaos in the streets I had warned him about.

* * *

Several months later, I received a call from the State Department informing me that Czechoslovakia's ambassador wanted to see me at his embassy in Washington. I went to see him, wondering what had prompted him to contact me through the State Department. His purpose, it seemed, was to extend an invitation for me to visit his country and help build a bridge for American companies to establish roots.

"You don't really want me," I said with a smile. "I'm a rabble-rouser."

The ambassador chuckled as I continued. "Seriously, I do try to make a little ruckus when I'm visiting a non-capitalist country. I want to talk about freedom, free enterprise, and capitalism. If I come to Prague, I want to talk to your political hierarchy about these topics. I want to talk to members of your press to try to explain it to them. But mostly, I want to talk to your students. And I want to talk to them about helping to make change."

He leaned across the table toward me and said in a firm, quiet tone, "Dr. Lesher, that is why you are being invited. We know you—and we know what you will say."

I immediately understood why I had been contacted in this roundabout manner—the Ambassador had clearly heard about my pro-democracy speeches in China and he hoped I would give similar talks in his country. In 1989, Czechoslovakia was teetering between its Communist Block past and a present edging toward possible social, political, and economic reform, though it was impossible to know how things would play out in the volatile environment.

Only two years prior, the secretary of the Communist Party in the country, Gustav Husak, decided to follow the political and economic reform path known as perestroika, paved by Soviet Union President Mikhail Gorbachev. Translated as "restructuring," perestroika allowed for greater independence in the marketplace and was intended to aid Soviet consumers. Ironically, it eventually contributed to the collapse of the Soviet Union into separate, highly nationalistic republics.

At the time, perestroika represented a glimmer of hope and increased freedom to the repressed citizenry of Czechoslovakia. But the government's new leadership wanted to move slowly, advocating only minor changes in the state's economic system in the immediate future and recommitting to the principles of socialism—even though the Iron Curtain was falling in Poland and East Germany, and the Soviet Union was dissolving. The minor changes made by Czech leadership did not sit well with a vast swath of the population, which watched a constant barrage of images from the West and the United States, depicting a better way of life in free, capitalist societies.

The seeds of discontent produced a huge demonstration in 1987 of Czech Catholics, who signed a petition for religious freedom. One year later, the country's first demonstration against Communist rule took place, with a crowd of several thousand protesting for religious, social, and political freedom. The peaceful display was broken up forcefully by police and many dissidents were arrested. But later in 1988, similar demonstrations swept through Prague and several other cities, followed by continued protests in 1989, starting in January and occurring in August and October.

It was in the spring of 1989 that I met with the Czech ambassador and he informed me of his desire that I travel to his country to speak to students. Clearly, he and others in the pro-reform segment of government saw me as one who might make a convincing case for capitalism—to a very receptive audience of Czech students, who were driving the demonstrations sweeping their nation.

"We know you can make that speech," the ambassador added. "If I made it, I'd go to jail."

"Can you promise I won't?" I interjected.

"We'll make sure of that," he replied, smiling.

As an historic footnote, Shirley Temple Black, America's former childhood sweetheart of the big and small screen, was appointed as America's ambassador to Czechoslovakia shortly after my under-the-radar meeting with the Czech ambassador. She came to meet me at the Chamber and have an informal chat about her new post. She had been briefed about my impending visit to Prague and remarked, "I look forward to seeing you there."

In October, 1989, I flew into Prague on my mission to promote our capitalist system and hopefully instigate change. I was delighted that Ambassador Black held a reception for me the evening before my first scheduled appearance. But interestingly, she excused herself after greeting me at the door, explaining she felt ill, and went upstairs for the rest of the evening. I was and remain convinced that she feigned being sick to keep herself an arm's length away from me. If my talks exploded into a controversy, she didn't want to be caught in the middle of it.

Her desire to steer clear of me made no difference in the situation, though I found it somewhat disappointing. The next day, as planned, I met with the Czechoslovakian press corps—both print and broadcast—and presented my talk, answering questions afterwards from the large media corps. My next stop was to a government hall to meet with political leaders—to deliver the same speech, but in greater detail.

Then, a day later, came the highlight: a speech to students at the Prague School of Economics. The small auditorium was packed to capacity with dozens of students and buzzing with an unmistakable air of excitement. I couldn't wait to deliver my talk—the first lecture, I was informed, devoted to freedom and free enterprise at the school in more than forty years. Most of the students spoke English and fully understood the message and points I conveyed.

Where exactly I fit into the swift progression of events in Czechoslovakia I do not know. But I gave that lecture with every ounce of conviction I had, and afterwards students surrounded me to ask questions. The first one I got was, "Is perestroika real for us here in Czechoslovakia?"

I thought for a moment and then answered, "Probably the best way to answer you is to say, I'm here. Would I be here speaking to you if it weren't for the fact that perestroika is beginning to take hold, even in Czechoslovakia?"

Only several weeks after I returned to Washington, events rapidly accelerated in Eastern Europe. On November 3, 1989, the Berlin Wall officially fell. Then, on November 17, Prague police in riot gear quelled a demonstration by students, but the spark had been lit, leading to more demonstrations. An estimated five hundred thousand protesters amassed in the city on November 20, and four days later, the leaders of Czechoslovakia's Communist Party resigned in what would be known as the Velvet Revolution—a transition of power with no violence. It officially ended on December 29, 1989, marking the end of Communist rule in the country after forty-one years and beginning the transition to a parliamentary form of government.

I watched the events unfold from Washington, DC, with a sense of awe and delight, knowing that another door to freedom had opened. And a part of me wondered if my remarks had provided an additional impetus for the students to mobilize and force the Communist government out of power.

One of the students who lingered to ask more questions, before the dean dispersed the group that day, was named Lubos Halousek. He had been particularly energized by my speech, and we exchanged addresses and corresponded for several years. In the first letter I sent him soon after the speech, I asked him about the prelude to my appearance and the post-script. He wrote back, "One of my fellow classmates told me, 'After hearing Dr. Lesher, we must go ahead and you must be part of this.' I agreed, but my younger brother went home and told my family. After that, they said if I got in trouble they would stop payment for my education. That meant I couldn't be a leader in the movement, I had to be a foot soldier."

But Lubos suggested in his letter that my speech absolutely pushed his fellow students forward in their commitment to force a change of government. He stressed that nearly all the students who attended my lecture were in the front lines of the revolution. I may never know what part my comments may have played, but I remained curious over the ensuing years and decided to reach out to see if I could locate Lubos. Agnes found his email on the Internet in the winter of 2016 and I e-mailed him, wondering how he remembered my visit and what kind of impact—through the lens of history—he thought it may have had. I wondered if he would get my message and write back. To my great pleasure, he did indeed. Here is what Lubos wrote:

Dear Dr. Lesher:

As you said, the change had been in the air already. There were some demonstrations in 1988 and 1989 in Prague, which in the years before would have been unthinkable. And all around us, the old regimes were collapsing. So, one could see that the seemingly eternal Soviet empire could come to its end even in this country. My parents raised me in a peaceful anti-communist way so I was getting excited feeling the "wind of change." Your speech came as a further step showing us that the change was going on. Never before one could have heard words like yours in normal public, i.e. beyond any meeting of dissidents, at least as far as I know. It was a real surprise to attend an assembly like this.

I do know that your speech really got me excited and I had to ask something which normally I would not have asked because I would have been afraid of being expelled out of the university. My friends say the question was followed by murmur.

It is evident that your speech helped in encouraging the people who attended it. Me and one of my best friends who attended the speech, we took part in the first demonstration crushed down severely by special police troops which started the Velvet Revolution. Many students were there, from all the Prague universities. The demonstration, or its illegal part with some 10,000 thousand participants, was organized by an underground students organization. I do not remember how we got in contact with them. i.e. how we knew that something was going to happen that evening. But sure our attitudes were changing very quickly and radicalizing.

There were many injured and one mistakenly suspected dead, which evoked a strong and quick reaction of other students, artists, and gradually of all the rest of the society. Only a brutal power could have destroyed the movement and save the old regime, at that point. Me and my friends were definitely no leaders, but we kept being active participants of the events from the very first hours until the resignation of the communist government. Should you have any more questions I would be happy to reply.

Best regards
Lubos

Six months after the change of power in 1989, I traveled to Bloomington, Indiana, the home of Indiana University, where I had earned my doctorate degree. I had the honor of giving a speech on May 4, 1990, to the MBA graduation ceremony in the Graduate School of Business Administration.

After brief opening remarks, I got to the heart of my talk, making the same points I had underscored so recently to students in China and Czechoslovakia.

"We live in the most exciting period in all of history," I said. "A period where we can safely predict that the next ten years will be the most competitive decade in all of history—a period of international competition as more countries convert to private enterprise. And we can be sure there will be more total economic growth than in any similar period in history."

Of course, knowing the value of a well-placed joke, I quickly added, "By the way, I have some reputation in international business. Some time ago, I was quoted on the front page of the *Wall Street Journal* when I said, 'It's easy for America to solve her problems with Japan—we let Japan send us as many cars as they like, as long as they take a lawyer back in exchange for each one.'"

Then I turned to the essence of my presentation. These were just some of those remarks:

"Day after day, we read of the exciting changes in all parts of the world as the human spirit seeks and demands freedom.

"Many of us are old enough to remember the relentless conquest of socialism and communism for more than thirty-five years after World War II. It seemed like every month we could see another map of the world with more and more countries colored in 'red.'

"But things are changing! Earlier this year, I visited Bolivia and Paraguay—two of our newest democracies. Everyone knows what has happened in Eastern Europe, but few seem to have noticed that the move to democracy is even more pronounced in our own hemisphere. . . . Ten years ago, less than 35 percent of the 347 million people in Latin America lived in countries with democratically elected governments. Today, with the recent events in Panama, Haiti and Nicaragua—98 percent of the people in Central and South America can vote. Cuba is the only holdout.

"The American business community, with the leadership of the US Chamber of Commerce, deserves some of the credit for these incredible changes. Americans trade and invest all over the world . . .

"We forget mankind has lived in poverty throughout history. Income per capital worldwide hardly changed from the time Christ walked the earth until this country was founded. And it's only been in this century—and especially the last forty years—where we have witnessed rapid increases in the standard of living. That progress has been in those countries where the values of private property, individual liberty, and self-initiative are respected and preserved."

I detailed my experiences with students leading the seismic events in China and Czechoslovakia, and then I turned my focus to the students seated before me.

"You've been blessed with intelligence and talent or you wouldn't be graduating with an MBA from one of the world's finest institutions. Celebration of achievement—which is our purpose here today—is truly enjoyable. The world is full of challenge and meeting challenges can be a very rewarding experience, as you have already discovered.

"Know that there are few limits—if you apply what you have already learned with energy. Know also that hard work can be its own reward.

"Most importantly, put something back—for your school, your family, your community. That, too, is a well-established IU tradition."

I thought of myself as I penned those words. In so many ways, they mirrored the life I had led—striving to succeed from an early age through difficult circumstances with little means or amenities; learning to rely on my own wits, energy, and determination to set a different path from my father; and embracing hard work and education to open new doors to the future.

Yet whatever I was fortunate enough to achieve was accompanied by a sense of responsibility, a desire to use my knowledge and experience to help other people—whether simply assisting friends or acquaintances with an idea for creating opportunities for success, or helping organizations, heads of foreign governments, and idealistic students living in oppression and dreaming of a better life.

That life—as you know by now I believe with every ounce of my being—is reached through freedom and the right to create one's own path to success and satisfaction in a free-enterprise system. My challenging childhood—from the L-shaped house in Chambersburg to the uncertainty that perpetually hovered over my hard-working, loving mother and my sister and me—didn't point to a career that would one day put me in the presence of US presidents and at the apex of dramatic world change. But our country's system allowed me the possibility to chart my own course. I did so fueled by traits honed amid adversity: toughness, self-reliance, and relentless desire to rise above my circumstances. And it was a course that ultimately led me to the defining and most rewarding period of my life, doing all I could to transform the US Chamber and infuse it with unparalleled clout on the business and political stage.

11 A New Fight—and New Direction

*T*HROUGHOUT HIS YEARS *at the helm of the Chamber, Dick Lesher found himself in more tense showdowns with bristling congressional leaders than he could count. Holding his ground with an innate toughness and fending off challenges came with the territory, especially for a man who had set out to orchestrate a broad change in the way the organization did business, always guided by what those close to him lauded as a straight-shooting, evenhanded style. As he entered his third different decade as the Chamber's top administrator in the early 1990s, trouble loomed on the horizon with a new fight—and this was one that would take its toll.*

But all the while, the people who worked for Lesher saw an entirely different side of the man in charge: a compassionate, just, and supportive leader who genuinely cared about his staff.

Among staff members who knew Lesher best during these years were Larry Kraus, vice president and general counsel at the US Chamber of Commerce (1978–1998); Meryl Comer, moderator of It's Your Business *(1983–1997); and Lonnie Taylor, vice president for congressional affairs and chief lobbyist for the US Chamber of Commerce (1993–2001). Each saw their boss in a different light from his occasionally pugnacious persona.*

Taylor, for one, will never forget his first interview with Lesher. He had been serving in the George H. W. Bush administration, working with elected officials on state, local, and regional levels as associate administrator for congressional and intergovernmental affairs in the US General Services Administration. But when Bush left office, Taylor found himself in the job market and wound up in Lesher's office, seeking a position of congressional lobbyist. He recalls it vividly:

"I'll never forget my job interview with Dick. I've been through many job interviews, though not because I've switched jobs frequently. I recall his with particular fondness. It wasn't so much of an interview as it was a chat. He made you feel very comfortable, almost as if he was inviting you into his living room.

"First, he asked about my family and about my mother in particular. She was my hero and he wanted to know why. I explained that she was such a tremendous role model as a woman who was widowed at an early age, but raised eleven children beautifully and put us all through school, later became a teacher and, upon retirement, became a loving foster mother who adopted three sisters."

During the course of the interview, Lesher wanted to know what kind of hobbies Taylor had.

"Do you ever go hunting?" he asked.

"No," Taylor replied.

"Do you play tennis?"

"No."

"Are you an active sportsman?"

"No."

Lesher chuckled over that, as if it gave him a big kick that apparently he and his interview subject had absolutely no pursuits in common. *"Well, gee,"* he finally said. *"You don't do anything, do you?"*

"I'm more focused on work as an activity," Taylor explained, wondering if his chances at the job had suddenly swirled down the drain.

Lesher looked at him, still smiling, and remarked, *"Well, we have to change that."*

Taylor got the job, and continued to marvel at Lesher's natural talent for putting people at ease. *"Dick and I later went together to Capitol Hill and met with a fair share of luminaries in both the House and Senate, and got into somewhat heated discussions on policy matters. But Dick was always the kind of guy who could instill a sense of calmness and ease in any of these talks—on any business issue.*

Lesher's gift for connecting with people was also reflected in Meryl Comer's recollection of their relationship. Throughout her seventeen years moderating It's Your Business, she always insisted on calling her boss by his formal title.

"Out of respect, I always referred to him as Dr. Lesher, on screen and off. His style of leadership was paternalistic—he saw the Chamber and its employees more like family, which I think is somewhat unique. It's certainly not common today at all. His supportive style of leadership built strong loyalties among staff members, many of whom stayed on the job for years. This was one of his signatures at the Chamber, whether it was the people who helped maintain the building or the senior executives.

"Even with all of his achievements, he was a very modest man, unlike many CEOs running high-powered organizations. But you had to respect a man who could persuade a board of business leaders, many of whom prefer not to talk to the press, to undertake such a bold television initiative. That's quite an accomplishment in itself, and it became a hallmark of his tenure."

The words of Larry Kraus, who started at the Chamber four years before Lesher arrived, shed light on the enormous stylistic change in leadership the new president created.

"First of all, Dick infused the Chamber with a completely different style of management. He brought professional, modern management techniques. He discarded many of the old rules and regulations that had governed how we operated, and modernized how we hired and evaluated people. Prior to this, the Chamber

was a heavily bureaucratic, buttoned-up organization with the same processes in place since its founding in 1912—I'm not joking. It was an organization that never took risks, never showed much initiative, and never enjoyed any real growth. It was stagnant and rigid.

"Early on, Dick focused on the substance of the programs that we were involved in. The Chamber was and is an advocacy organization and he wanted us to be at the forefront of advocacy."

But Kraus was equally impressed with Lesher as a person, and head of an organization of many competing egos and diverse skillsets.

"He was always very self-reliant and self-assured, but not in a cocky way. As a leader, he was incredibly fair—probably one of the fairest people I have ever dealt with. He would always listen to opposing points of view. He and I didn't agree on a whole host of things, but he was open to ideas and criticism. And he was a joy to work with. As we would say, he was the kind of guy you'd want in the foxhole with you. He was tenacious, hard-working, and incredibly bright and inventive."

Nonetheless, trouble was brewing on the horizon at the outset of the Clinton aministration, and Lesher would soon find himself under attack from an unexpected and unrelenting source.

I look back on my years guiding the United States Chamber of Commerce with great satisfaction with what we implemented and accomplished at a pivotal point in history. There were so many organizations in Washington that simply blew in the wind, but I was so proud of the integrity of the Chamber's policy-making process—in addition to our achievements. One thing became clear during my time on the job: whatever the issue was and whoever was in the White House, the first order of business was to try to get the support of the Chamber on any business or economic issue.

Many people make the mistake of thinking that the Chamber is a Republican organization. Actually, it is an independent organization (and I was always a registered Independent). We have many Democrats in our two hundred twenty-five thousand companies and our goal was always to represent the business interests. Sometimes, we wound up helping Republicans; sometimes Democrats. If a member of Congress wanted our endorsement, all he or she had to do was vote with us 70 percent of the time.

Our power was built on several pillars: the National Chamber Alliance for Politics, through which we made endorsements based on voting records of members of Congress; the National Chamber Litigation Center, which established an extremely high batting average in cases we took to court; the Spirit of Enterprise initiative, which resulted in grassroots efforts of thousands of committees ready to write letters and make phone calls if we asked them to; and—the endeavor that tied everything together—the communications operation, the most sophisticated one ever put together by an organization of this kind. It created a tangible method for the Chamber to influence opinions and policies, but also created an important perception of power.

But in the early 1990s, there was a tangible shift in the country's political atmosphere that made our mission more challenging. I began to grow weary of the bitter tone overtaking Washington politics, even within the Republican Party whose policies were so closely aligned with those of the Chamber. I incurred the wrath of certain members of the right when I agreed to collaborate with Clinton, at the outset of his presidency, on key economic policies. As the *Wall Street Journal* noted, "After President Clinton's election in 1992, House Republican leaders—then in the minority—blasted Mr. Lesher and his top lobbyist, William Archey, for being too supportive of the new Democratic president."

I was, in fact, initially open to the idea of the health care proposal pushed by the Clinton administration. Health care had been a major problem in the country for decades; rates had risen higher because of over-use and abuse of the system and the actions of trial lawyers who won huge settlements for any type of malfunction. The price of liability insurance rocketed through the roof, driving many single practitioners out of business into group practices, changing the whole face of medicine. By the 1990s, solving the health care problem was a high priority on everybody's list, Democrats, Republicans, and the business community.

It's important to understand that the first version of the healthcare program, proposed by then First Lady Hillary Clinton, was acceptable to us because she promised no mandates, with voluntary participation, and no financial burden on businesses. The Chamber had been looking for a solution to healthcare for many years and this sounded promising, so we told Mrs. Clinton that we would work with her. But when the provision for no mandates was pulled off the table, the business community—including us—railed against her plan and worked to defeat it. Unfortunately, by this point, the Chamber was already identified as a supporter and we never escaped the stigma of having tried to work with the Clintons at the outset.

That said, I had no regrets in being willing to work with Clinton at the outset, as my comment in that same *WJS* story expressed: "I think we did the right thing. He came in as a new-style Democrat making a lot of promises to business. We gave him the benefit of the doubt. When we saw some of the things he proposed, we opposed him." Of course, we helped Clinton pass NAFTA with support from most of the Republicans in Congress. We also worked with the Clinton administration to push welfare reform through Congress, a program that contained "workfare" and training elements.

In 1993, powerful, hardline House members of the Republican Party who had taken control of the House of Representatives were furious that I did not openly oppose a president they disliked intensely—and sharpened their attacks on me as a result. Dick Army and Tom DeLay even circulated a letter that took note of a "rapidly spreading frustration and anger with the Chamber's failure to take an aggressive posture on the Clinton economic program." All of a sudden, the hardliners were the big boys in town and they intended to push aside anybody who disagreed with them. They even got into fighting among themselves as well.

Nothing made this wing of the party angrier with me than the fact that the Chamber allowed Clinton to use our television studios to tape educational messages. What they failed to acknowledge was that we had a contract with the Department of Education to handle a number of educational initiatives. During the administration of George H. W. Bush, the president taped these spots in our studios and it was never an issue. When Clinton was elected, our contract with the Department of Education was still in effect, so naturally we allowed the new president to use our studios, too. I visited with him while he was there and we chatted amiably, like two normal human beings. But news stories or TV spots would report that Clinton had visited the US Chamber to participate in a television program—without explaining that it was sponsored by the Department of Education. And every time a story about that appeared, the Republican elite went ballistic.

My response was, "Wait a minute. Did you ever hear of a contract? Did you ever hear that Clinton is president?" My explanations of our contractual responsibility didn't satisfy my critics for one second. I didn't elect Clinton, but I chose to deal with him and the situation just grew uglier. It was hard to swallow: to work so hard and then to have those same Republicans who had backed me become antagonistic for simply honoring our education contract. The Chamber helped make Gingrich, providing him with many opportunities to address audiences in our building. He wrote the foreword to one of my books, *Meltdown on Main Street*. But he was suddenly against me because my organization was dealing with a president that he and many Republicans despised.

The bottom line in all of this: after the Republicans took control of the House in 1994, they were no longer happy with the best friend they'd ever had, the US Chamber. Because we didn't do things exactly how they wanted, they screamed to high heaven—and were treating their opponents in Congress even more badly. The animosity so prevalent in today's politics—the ill will between parties—can be traced back to that group of Republicans, not the Democrats. From then on, there is no question that people in their ranks were gunning for me. At one point, I even was summoned to the House to meet with about thirty members of this cadre of powerful GOP lawmakers, and it was as if they were holding pitchforks, aimed at me.

Still, I stood my ground in the face of their bluster and vitriol. And in 1997, I retired on my own terms, knowing I had done everything in my power to elevate the business community. I came into the job at a time when the prevailing image of business was negative, following years of war and political scandal. I feel immense satisfaction that we enhanced that image—and created a new level of respect and recognition—through all of our programs. Along the way, we worked with presidential administrations on many important issues, including the prevention of drugs in the work place initiatives undertaken by the Reagan and Bush White Houses. And I did everything I could to spread the message of free enterprise to foreign students living amid oppression, hungering for hope and opportunity.

I feel compelled to add that it is simply amazing to me that some people and politicians still think that socialism is better than capitalism. Socialism has been tried in many countries and failed, and was discarded in most. In some regions, it was as though the world was conducting laboratory experiments to test which system was best: socialism or capitalism. Many countries with the same history, culture, and natural resources had differing systems, and offer striking contrasts in the effects on the economy. For example, in Mainland China versus Taiwan, Singapore and Hong Kong, or North Korea versus South Korea, and East Germany versus West Germany, the free market produced as much as twenty times greater income per capita and consequently a twenty times better standard of living than those with central planning and government control of markets.

In a world that has become increasingly frightening and uncertain—faced today with an ever-growing global threat of terrorism—spreading the message of economic freedom has never been more important. It was a privilege to be positioned in my career to do that, to work with and meet so many interesting and gifted individuals along the way—whether I agreed with them or not.

Some of our signature initiatives—most notably our national television show—were not continued after my departure. Nor was the monthly magazine that predated my arrival, *Nation's Business.* We were slightly in the red for both our television operation and magazine, but definitely close enough to push both enterprises into substantial profit.

Now, two decades after my retirement, they are spending more money on a new publication than they would have with *Nation's Business*—and the publication doesn't have the track record and respect of the one that was discontinued. It's hard for me to understand why they would want to discard two assets of such value, and which, in the case of *It's Your Business,* was so hard to achieve in the first place. And it's only natural for these actions to be disappointing, given all we did to create a high profile that made the Chamber a genuine presence in the Congress, the White House and the business world, and among foreign leaders as well. The entire TV operation was an extremely powerful vehicle for influencing Congress and the White House.

Despite my difference in philosophy, I certainly wish the organization I was honored to lead the best in all it does. I'm proud that I left behind a very strong organization—including a reserve amounting to fifty million dollars, zero debt, a massive building, and all of its improvements already paid for.

Suffice it say, the Chamber, and its mission to lobby for business, is in my blood and that will never change. I have immeasurable pride in our democratic way of life. I was, and remain, an advocate for individuals and businesses to prosper without interference from expanding government encroachment on their lives with increased regulations and tax hikes.

As I mentioned at the start of this book, Thomas Jefferson stated that it's the natural order for government to grow, and liberty to yield. We've seen that trend since the United States was founded, with government growing progressively bigger ever since. I believe we need to work steadfastly to push back against that tide so private enterprise can thrive without endless, government-imposed red tape. That tenet guided me in all I did as president of the Chamber.

The fight I undertook on behalf of business and free enterprise still needs to be fought today and in the future. President Reagan addressed that dynamic in his last speech to us at the Chamber. He told us: "I'm leaving now, but you must carry on, because this challenge will be never-ending."

I for one will never stop speaking up for free enterprise, or being thankful that I was able to do so—loud and clear—on the national and international platform. When I reflect on the road I have traveled since I thumbed rides as a child, it's hard to believe the turns my life has taken. I could never have imagined that the little boy who grew up in a difficult Depression-era household would one day earn a doctorate while working all night and supporting a growing family, eventually rise to a top leadership position in NASA when we put a man on the moon and eventually work with presidents, members of Congress, and heads of state—more than 60 all told—as president of the Chamber.

Time and time again, history has proven that people thrive in systems built on a foundation of economic opportunity. I have been a proud crusader for that capitalist way for much of my adult life. I thank you for accompanying me through the pages of this journey—and I hope the experience has been as enjoyable and fulfilling for you as it has been for me.

RICHARD LESHER earned his doctorate at Indiana University and was President of the United States Chamber of Commerce from 1975 to 1997.

DAVE SCHEIBER is an award-winning journalist and the coauthor of five books, including *Covert: My Years Infiltrating the Mob* (chronicling the life of undercover agent Bob Delaney and named a Best Book of 2008 by *USA Today*).

www.ingramcontent.com/pod-product-compliance
Lightning Source LLC
Chambersburg PA
CBHW050842270326
41930CB00019B/3437